LINUX FOR BEGINNERS

A step-by-step guide to learn architecture, installation, configuration, basic functions, command line and all the essentials of Linux, including manipulating and editing files

Julian James McKinnon

© **Copyright 2020 - All rights reserved.**

The content contained within this book may not be reproduced, duplicated or transmitted without direct written permission from the author or the publisher.
Under no circumstances will any blame or legal responsibility be held against the publisher, or author, for any damages, reparation, or monetary loss due to the information contained within this book. Either directly or indirectly.

Legal Notice:

This book is copyright protected. This book is only for personal use. You cannot amend, distribute, sell, use, quote or paraphrase any part, or the content within this book, without the consent of the author or publisher.

Disclaimer Notice:

Please note the information contained within this document is for educational and entertainment purposes only. All effort has been executed to present accurate, up to date, and reliable, complete information. No warranties of any kind are declared or implied. Readers acknowledge that the author is not engaging in the rendering of legal, financial, medical or professional advice. The content within this book has been derived from various sources. Please consult a licensed professional before attempting any techniques outlined in this book.

By reading this document, the reader agrees that under no circumstances is the author responsible for any losses, direct or indirect, which are incurred as a result of the use of the information contained within this document, including, but not limited to, — errors, omissions, or inaccuracies.

Table of Contents

Introduction 6

Chapter1: Basic Background 10

Chapter 2: The Architecture of Linux 22

Chapter 3: Installation Basics 42

Chapter 4: Linux Distributions 63

Chapter 5: GNU Utilities 79

Chapter 6: The Shell 83

Chapter 7: Basic Functions of Linux 94

Chapter 8: Overview of Processes 106

Chapter 9: The Linux Processes 111

Chapter 10: Manual Pages 145

Chapter 11: Manipulating Files and Directories 150

Chapter 12: Advanced Working with Files 176

Chapte 13: Text Editors 189

Chapter 14 : Edit your Files using Vim 197

Chapter 15: Linux Softwares to Use 201

Conclusion 207

Introduction

Thank you for taking the time to pick up this book, that will teach you about the ins and outs of Linux.

Like anything in life, you expect something to work correctly the first time you use it.

You don't want to have to spend the extra time reading the manual and trying to figure out how it operates correctly.

For example, when you buy a car, most people don't care about how advanced this or that feature is.

You want to put the keys into the ignition and drive it like you would any other vehicle.

Then when you need to know something specific, you go to the manual for that specific information.

This book is meant to demonstrate what Linux can do for you, rather than wasting your time giving you lots of boring data that you probably won't care to remember.

If you need more information about something, then you can use the basic understanding that you have, and do a deeper investigation of how the command works.

I have always discovered, when I have a basic foundational knowledge of anything, I will generally know where to look for or what questions to ask to get the information I need.

It is when I don't have that foundational knowledge, that I may not know where to start, which makes it a great deal more difficult.

There is a plethora of information out on the web or in other references that will go into much greater depth on most of the topics in the book than what I will be covering.

Although, most of us don't have the time or interest to read those references.

There are three ways to access a Linux system:

- Through a text console. In this method, the user connects directly to the computer that has Linux installed and then they can access it through a non-graphic system
- From a graphical session manager (X Window). Here the user connects directly to the computer that has Linux installed and accesses the system through a graphical program
- From a remote computer using telnet or secure shell.

In any of the previous situations, the following will appear (more or less):

- Login: (Username is typed)

- Password: (The password is typed, which is not visible on the screen)
  - For security reasons, the password must meet certain conditions such as:
    - Contain at least six characters
    - Contain at least one numerical or special character and two alphabetic characters
    - Be different from the login name

The first time the system is accessed, the password used will be the one provided by the administrator of the system.

There are several ways to end the work session in Linux, depending on whether we are in graphic mode or text.

In-text mode:

- Press the <ctrl> d keys
- Enter the exit command.

In graphic mode:

The output of X Window depends on the window manager that is running.

Can You Have Linux?

Linux can run on different types of computer systems, and because it is available on many distributions, you can choose the distribution that will allow you to install the operating system on the computer that you have available.

Currently, Linux can be installed on computers with the following processors:

- Hewlett-Packard HP PA RISC
- Alpha AXPs
- Motorola 68000 family
- MIPS R5x00 R4x00
- PowerPC and PowerPC64
- 64-bit AMD64 processors
- Intel 80x86 processors
- Pentium processors

My objective in writing this book is to provide you the quickest, and hopefully, most enjoyable introduction to Linux.

It is also meant to help you get started learning the OS more quickly by giving you a sampler platter of commands that you can try and see the results.

Once again, thanks for taking the time to read this book.

I hope you find learning all about the Linux operating system to be helpful and enjoyable.

Chapter1: Basic Background

Originally, Linux was developed merely as a hobby project by a programmer known as Linus Torvalds in the early 1990s while at the University Of Helsinki In Finland.

The project was inspired by a small Unix (an operating system) system called Minix that had been developed by professor Andy Tanenbaum who used the Unix code to teach students of that university about operating systems.

At that time, Unix was only used in universities for academic purposes.

The professor developed Minix (a little clone of Unix) to effectively teach his students about operating systems with a bit more depth.

Linus was inspired by Minix and developed his own clone, which he named Linux.

On 5th October 1991, version 0.02- which was the first version of Linux, was announced by Linus.

While this version was able to run the Bourne shell (bash)- the command line interface- and a compiler called GCC, there wasn't so much else to it.

Version 0.03 was released sometime later, and then the version number was bumped up to 0.10, as more people began embracing the software.

After a couple more revisions, Linus released version 0.95 in March 1992 as a way of reflecting his expectation that the system was prepared for an 'official' release real soon.

About one year and a half later (December 1993), the version was finally made it to 1.0.

Today, Linux is a total clone of Unix and has since been able to reach a user base spanning industries and continents.

The people who understand it see and appreciates its use in virtually everything- from cars to smartphones, home appliances like fridges, and supercomputers, this operating system is everywhere.

Linux runs the largest part of the internet, the computers making all the scientific breakthroughs you hear about every other day and the world's stock exchanges.

As you appreciate its existence, don't forget that this operating system was (and still is) the most secure, reliable, and hassle-free operating system available before it became the best platform to run servers, desktops, and embedded systems all over the globe.

With that short history, I believe you are now ready for some information to get you up to speed on this marvelous platform.

UNIX EVOLUTION

In this section, we'll be looking at Linux history.

Now when it comes to Linux history, even before I speak about what is the beginning of Linux or how Linux evolved, we need to look at the evolution of computers.

Evolution of Computers and UNIX

If you all know like when the computers were developed or introduced, they were very big, big size systems, non-affordable and I think when the computers were developed the first time they were as big as small houses that we have.

Pretty big systems and they were not so easy to be affordable by a normal person.

When the computers first started to evolve, every company had a different operating system, they used to buy the hardware, they used to create their own operating system, and they used to run the computers as per their own company norms.

With different companies buying in the hardware and different companies introducing their own operating system, the issue was each computer was developed for a specific purpose that means every system had a specific purpose like one server will have a specific purpose, one workstation will have a specific purpose, but there was no standardized operating system across all the systems or the servers or the workstations.

The problem was these systems were extremely costly because, in those days when computers were created initially, the hardware cost was very high.

If you compare this with mobile phones also initially when mobile phones were created and were very costly.

But now today if you see the demand is so high that the hardware costs have gone down and anyone can purchase a mobile phone.

The same is with computers.

Today you can get computers at an affordable price since many companies are creating computers, meaning lots of competition.

So when demand increases, when competition increases, definitely the prices will come down.

But when computers were first started, it was not easy for anyone to afford a computer and that's why only companies used to afford computers and they were extremely costly.

Also, in those days, it was a specific skill that was required to understand and learn computers.

So, for a normal person, it was impossible to learn and understand computers or operating systems.

Every company had skilled labor, skilled people who were able to operate and work on these specific computers.

So that's the main evolution of computers, and that's how it started.

Now understand this guy with this evolution; there was definitely a problem.

The problem is every company had its own monopoly when it comes to hardware or the computer's operating system.

They developed their own operating system.

So, there is no standardization of the operating system it comes to computers and the companies that build their own operating system.

That's why in 1969, a team of developers started at Bell Labs.

I'm not sure, but many of you might have heard about Bell Labs or Bell Laboratories.

That's where the C language was first developed.

That's the same lab where a team of developers thought why not build a standard operating system that can be used across computers so that people do not have to worry about the hardware nor the software.

Initially, the problem was the cost with regard to the hardware, and then there was another cost to build an operating system for specific computers.

To reduce that cost, the developers thought, why not create a standard operating system so that people can purchase standard hardware.

They can purchase or install the standard operating system and then continue the development or use their applications.

That's when it started, or that's the beginning of Unix.

The goal of the UNIX project was to create pretty common software for all the computers because all companies were developing their own operating system; it was a pretty hard job.

So they wanted to standardize the process.

With this in mind, the project was named as the UNIX and started to work towards one common goal, and that was to create a common software for all the computers.

The UNIX or the UNIX operating system was started on C language.

Now the team had a further goal when it comes to the development of the UNIX operating system, and the goal was to create a code that is easy to understand and reusable or recyclable.

This recyclable code is known as the kernel.

The kernel is the part of the operating system since an operating system has multiple components.

The kernel is responsible for communicating with the hardware and the software.

That's the part that is directly communicating with your computer hardware.

The kernel is recyclable and is used to develop the operating system and enhance the features.

What many people do NOW is use this kernel because it's standard code, and they can develop their own flavors of UNIX by modifying the kernel or the software that talks to the kernel or the applications that talk to the kernel because it is a standard layer.

Earlier, you had to develop an operating system that is speaking directly to the hardware.

Now you have a layer, the kernel, or a mediator responsible for speaking to the hardware.

So we need to create applications that can only speak directly to kernel because the kernel handles the communication with the hardware.

It was not a requirement to develop the applications that will speak directly to the hardware.

We have a standard layer of the kernel, so the applications will communicate with the kernel, which in turn will communicate with the hardware.

Another goal of this project was to develop the UNIX operating system with open source code.

This implies that the UNIX operating system code is open for anyone.

Anyone can read the kernel; anyone can modify as per their requirement and can use the kernel and build some other flavor of the UNIX operating system.

As UNIX was a complex operating system, in the beginning, it was only found in universities, government, organizations, and big corporates.

But then, as we have just seen that the source code for UNIX is open source, what happened is that companies like IBM-AIX, HP-UX, Sun Solaris started creating their own flavor of UNIX.

How Linux came into the picture

Being an initial operating system, the UNIX operating system was complex or pretty hard to configure.

Only big corporations can afford to use UNIX, modify, and use it for their own purpose.

There was this guy named Linus Torvalds.

He was a student in Finland, and his goal was to create or design a freely available academic version of UNIX.

In 1991, he started writing his code for his own PC.

That's how this project of Linux started.

There were no intentions to create a pretty big operating system that will challenge the UNIX operating system.

No, the goal was to create a freely available Academy version of UNIX, but he only wanted to create it for his Wizard system, and the main reason for doing this or this goal was because he was not able to afford the UNIX operating system.

So he had no idea about how big this project would become.

Initially what he did was because I think it might be because of his ego or as he was not able to afford the UNIX operating system, he created the Linux operating system free but restricted it for the commercial use because UNIX was commercial operating system and it was hard for people to use UNIX for their own purpose.

That's why he created Linux free like anyone can use it but not for commercial purposes.

So companies or the big corporations could not purchase or use the Linux operating system for their own purpose.

In 1992, he released Linux under GNU- General Public License.

Today any company can use the Linux operating system because it's completely free. You don't need to have a license.

Nowaday's Linux is almost everywhere.

It is used in Supercomputers, Laptops, Tablets, Mobiles, and Routers, Washing machines, Watches, Servers, Cars, etc. almost everywhere.

Linux features

Multi-User Operating System

Multiple users can connect to the same operating system from different terminals and utilize the hardware resources like RAM, Hard disk, and work on the operating system simultaneously.

So it's not like one user is connected to the operating system, and the other user will not be able to connect to the operating system until the first user logs out.

Multiple users can connect to the same operating system and work on the Linux Operating System.

Multi-Tasking

Multi-tasking means the tasks or the system calls or the user requests inside the Linux operating system; it is so intelligent that it is able to divide the tasks and work on multiple tasks based on the CPU threads.

So all the tasks are divided, and they are executed parallelly when it comes to CPU threads.

Multiple CPU threads will execute multiple user requests, and that's why this term multitasking came into the picture.

Portability

Portability does not mean that you can take the Linux operating system in your pen drive or on a CD, of course, you can do that, but the main point when it comes to portability is you can install Linux on any hardware,

It's so easy like we have just now seen the places where we can find the Linux operating system.

So that means Linux is easily portable onto different types of hardware.

Security

Like inside Linux, we have authentication.

When you try to connect to the Linux operating system, you definitely need to provide the user ID and password.

When you try to access files, then you have what they are called permissions.

You need to have the permissions in order to access the file, and again, the files can be encrypted inside the operating system so that it converts it into a format that is not readable when someone else tries to open it who doesn't have the permissions.

GUI Interface

We can also have Linux operating system where if you install some packages, you can use Linux in GUI.

Note: The Mac operating system is built on Unix OS.

File System

A file system allows you to arrange your files and directories in a systematic order.

Open Source

It means anyone can freely download, install, and use the Linux operating system.

Chapter 2: The Architecture of Linux

Before we are able to get into some of the cool codes and learn more about what we can do with the Linux system, we first need to take a look at what Linux is.

While this may not quite have the name recognition that we are going to find with some of the other operating systems out there, like Mac and Windows, you will find that Linux is creating its own niche and becoming more popular each day.

That is why we need to spend some time learning more about this and what we are able to do with it overall.

From cars to smartphones, home applications and supercomputers, enterprise servers to home desktops, this operating system is going to be all around us.

This is a newer operating system in some respects, and it came out around the mid-1990s.

Since that time, it has been able to reach a big user-base that is found throughout the globe.

In fact, we are going to find that Linux is found, in one form or another, all around us.

Linux is versatile and a great option to work with, so you will find that it is going to be inside a lot of the options that you use regularly.

For example, many phones are going to have Linux inside of them.

Also, it is going to be found in thermostats, in cars, Roku devices, televisions, cars and so much more.

And it is also responsible for running much of what we can find on the Internet, so that is a big plus as well.

But, outside of being one of the platforms of choice to help out with a lot of the work that needs to be done with embedded systems, servers and even desktops that are found throughout the world, Linux is going to have a lot of benefits that we can rely on as well.

For example, when it is compared to some of the other operating systems that are out there, it is one of the most reliable, worry-free, and secure options that you can choose.

With some of this in mind, it is time for us to go through and learn a bit more about some of the parts that come with this operating system, and how we can use these for our own benefit as well.

Here is all of the information that you need to know as someone new to the Linux platform.

What is Linux?

The first thing that we need to take a look at is the fact that Linux is going to be an operating system.

It is similar to the operating systems that we use like Mac OS, iOS, and Windows.

In fact, one of the most popular platforms that is found on the planet, Android, is going to be powered thanks to the Linux operating system.

Linux operating system is one of the most sophisticated operating systems out there.

It is available in Computers, Tablets, Watches, and Phones, etc.

To break this down, the operating system is simply going to be a type of software that is going to be able to manage all of the resources of the hardware that are associated with your laptop or desktop.

To keep it simple, the operating system is going to help manage all of the communication that happens between the hardware and the software.

If you did not have an operating system in place, then the software would not be able to function the way that you would like.

You will find that, just like some of the other operating systems that are out there, the Linux operating system is going to come in with a few different pieces that we need to work with.

Some of these are going to include:

- Bootloader: This is going to be the software that is able to manage the boot process on our computer.

    For most users, this is going just to be the splash screen that is going to pop up and then will go away when you are first booting up into the operating system.

- Kernel: This is going to be the one piece of the whole that is called Linux.

    This is going to be the core of our system and it is responsible for managing the memory peripheral devices and CPU.

    The kernel is going to be the bottom level that we will find with our operating system.

- Init system: This is going to be one of the sub-systems that are going to bootstrap the user space, and then it will be in control of the daemons.

    One of the most widely used of these is going to be a system, which is also sometimes seen as the most controversial of them.

This is going to be the system that is responsible for booting up the operating system, once the initial booting is handed over from the initial bootloader that we use.

- Daemons: These are going to be some of the background services.

  It could include options like scheduling, sound, and printing, but you can move them around to fit your needs.

  They are either going to start up when you do a boot of the system, or after you have had a chance to log into the desktop.

- Shell- You've probably also heard this word too many times as well or the Linux command line, which at one time scared many people away from Linux (perhaps because they thought they had to learn some mind-numbing command line structure to use the OS).

  The shell is the command process that lets you control your computer through commands by typing them into a text interface.

Today, you can work with Linux without even touching the command line, but it's important to work with it, as we are going to see shortly.

- Graphical server: This is going to be the sub-system that will display all of the different graphics that you want on the monitor.

  It is called X or the x server.

- Desktop environment: This is going to be the piece of the operating system that you are actually going to spend time interacting with.

  This is the actual implementation of the metaphor 'desktop' that is made of programs running on the visible surface of the operating system that you will interact with directly.

  There are going to be a lot of options for this kind of environment that we can choose from, including Cinnamon, Xfce, gnome, utility, Pantheon Enlightenment, and more.

  Each of these environments is going to include some of the applications that you need built-in, including the games, web browsers, configuration tools, file managers, and more.

- Applications: The desktop environment that you choose is not going to come with a ton of applications for you to choose from.

  Instead, it is going to be necessary for you to go out and search for the software titles that you want, and then you can find them and install them for your needs.

  For example, Ubuntu Linux is going to have what is known as the Ubuntu Software Center, which is going to help you go through thousands of apps, and then install the ones that you like the most, from one centralized location.

  Linux provides thousands of software titles, which you can easily access and install, which is the same case with Windows and Mac.

Linux is pretty much famous among the developers and IT companies because when it comes to Windows, you might have heard about viruses.

A virus is a program that works out of control of the user.

Now the beauty with Linux is that there is nothing called a virus.

It is a very sophisticated operating system, and there is nothing like you need to download antivirus or you need to find some viruses.

This makes Linux a wonderful operating system to use in IT companies and servers.

Structure of the Linux Operating System

Before I get into the different parts or the different components that make the Linux operating system, we need to understand that any operating system whether it is Linux, Windows, Unix or HP any operating system, it is a collection of specific functions or it is a collection of multiple components, and each component has a designated or a specific function.

For example, in a company we have multiple departments, and each department has designated work to do.

In the same way in operating systems, we have multiple components or the software components that are designed to perform specific functions.

Now will be discussing all the main components inside the Linux operating system.

Linux kernel

Linux Kernel is the core of the Linux operating system.

It is responsible for communicating between the hardware.

In your systems or any of the desktop, laptop, or server, you have the hardware devices like your CD reader, USB port, HDMI port, LAN port, and memory card readers.

All these are devices that are attached to your laptop.

The kernel is responsible for speaking to these devices using machine language.

Machine language is nothing but 0s and 1s.

The hardware or the processor of the machine understands everything in 0s in 1s.

The kernel is more responsible in speaking to these devices in their own language and also speaks with the software.

Now inside the kernel, there are multiple responsibilities to be performed.

The kernel is also responsible for managing the system resources.

In your system, we know that we have RAM, Hard disk, processes that go in and we also have multiple devices attached to a system, and there are multiple user requests.

The kernel manages resources like how much RAM to be used, how much memory to be given, where to write on the hard disk, how to handle multiple user requests, which device to activate for a specific purpose.

All these are under resource management.

Below are some Resources:

<u>Memory Management</u>

The kernel checks two applications that need memory or the one requesting RAM then determines how much memory is to be given to which application and decides the application to get priority when it comes to RAM allocation.

Process Management

Process Management is like we have multiple processes; every application will have a background process that will be running.

So which process will get priority?

Technically the memory is assigned to processes, not the application.

So when you run an application, it initiates multiple background processes, and each background process will be assigned some memory.

Device management

Device Management is like which device, e.g., USB port, Webcam, LAN port, should be used and how it has to be used.

Handling System Calls

Handling System Calls is like if a user performs multiple requests, then which request to be handled first, which request to be handled second and third.

All those responsibilities go under the Linux Kernel.

System Libraries

Let us understand the system libraries in a different dimension.

See, we have the kernel, which is responsible for speaking with the system hardware.

The users will be running multiple applications on an Operating System.

The operating system needs to speak to the kernel.

It's impossible that we allow each application to speak directly to kernel because each application is developed by different persons or under different Technology.

For example, some applications are developed in Java, some in .Net.

So it becomes hard or tough to make sure that all the applications are directly able to speak with the kernel.

Now in this scenario, the operating system developers have created some free define programs.

These programs become the mediator between the kernel and the application so that it becomes easy for any developer just to pick up the system libraries and develop their application.

Let's look at how system libraries help Linux operating system:

The first one would be applications that need to communicate with the kernel.

Each application will try to communicate with the kernel, but it's hard if we allow different applications to communicate with the kernel directly.

So, in this case, the different applications will have issues to directly communicate with the kernel because each application is built or developed by different developers by using different technologies.

There is no standard when it comes to application development.

Anyone can use any technology to develop the application.

Consequently, because we have multiple applications developed in different technologies, we need a standard process or Standard System libraries.

So operating system developers have created standardized system libraries.

These libraries are nothing but predefined programs that are available inside the OS.

What they do is whenever they are building some applications, they will include these libraries, and each library will have a set of functions.

So they will include the libraries depending on their requirement, and these libraries are responsible for speaking with the kernel.

Now when we look at the process of communication flow, it looks something like below:

Applications >> System Libraries >> Kernel >> Hardware

System Tools

To run any operating system, we need some tools or predefined tools that help you navigate or work inside the operating system.

When you get the Windows operating system, we know that we have multiple tools that help us work with the operating system.

Like we have a Control Panel, Command Prompt that allows us to communicate directly with the operating system and so on.

So the commands that help you manage your operating system come under system tools.

These are not user tools.

There is a difference between system tools and user tools.

The user tools would be like Notepad, Paint, and MS - Office, so on.

The system tools would be your Control Panel, Device Driver Manager; all these come under system tools.

Basically, the system tools inside the Linux operating system, are the comments and tools that help you operate OS in a standard way.

These are the commands to change directory, create/open/delete files, move files, etc.

So all these comments that help you manage to administer your operating system come under system tools.

Whenever you install any operating system, the system tools are already developed by the operating system developers, and you can just use them to manage your operating system.

Development Tools

If you are a normal user of the Windows operating system, you already know that there are updates that come with the Windows operating system on a timely basis, and you need to update your operating system.

These updates are nothing but the bug fixes or other modifications that are done to the operating system and allows you to work faster or improve the operating system performance.

These developer tools are always available whenever it comes to any operating system; whether it is Windows, Linux, UNIX, all have the developer tools.

These developers' tools help developers create new OS applications.

They are created by the developers for the developers so that they can develop the OS level applications inside the operating system and make sure to release new updates to each operating system.

End-User Tool

End-user tools are the ones that will be used by the end-users would like Notepad, Paint, MS Office, Media player, Windows Browser, Web Browser, PowerPoint, and so on.

All these applications that are used by the end-users are known as End User Tools.

Why Should I Use Linux?

This is one of the first questions that a lot of people are going to ask when they first hear about the Linux system overall.

They may be curious as to why they should learn a completely new computing environment when the operating system that is already on their computer and was shipped to them when they ordered the device is working just fine.

Would it really be worth their time to learn a new one and see how it works?

To help us to answer this question, it is important to answer a few other questions to give us a good idea of what the Linux system can do for us that our traditional operating system is not able to do.

For example, does the operating system that you are currently using actually work just fine?

Or are you constantly dealing with a lot of obstacles like malware, viruses, slowdowns, costly repairs, licensing fees, and crashes all of the time?

If you find that these are things that you are dealing with regularly, especially once you have had the computer for some time, then you may find that the perfect platform for you to use to prevent some of this is going to be the Linux system.

It is one of the operating systems that has evolved to become one of the most reliable out of all of them.

And when you can combine all of that reliability with zero costs, you will end up with the perfect solution for the platform that you need.

That is right; you can get the Linux system and all of the benefits that come with it all together for free.

And you can take the Linux operating system and install it on as many computers as you would like, and use it as much as you would like, without having to worry about how much it will cost to use, how much the software is, and you also don't need to worry about server licensing.

We can also take a look at the cost of adding on a server in Linux compared to the Windows Server 2016.

The price of the Windows option for a standard edition is going to be about $882 if you purchase it right from Microsoft and not from another part.

This is not going to include any of the Client Access Licenses, and the licenses for all of the other software that you decide are important and need to be run in this as well, such as a mail server, web server, and a database.

For example, the single user who works with the CAL on the Windows system is going to cost you about $38.

But if you need to have a lot of users, that cost is going to go up pretty quickly.

If you need to work with ten people on the server, then you are going to end up with $380 just to do that part.

And that is just with the software licensing that you would like to get done.

But it is a bit different when we are working with the Linux server.

For the Linux option, you will be able to get all of that for free, and it is also easy for you to install.

In fact, being able to go through and add in a web server with all of the features, including a database server, is just going to take a few clicks or a few commands to get done.

This alone, especially for some of the bigger businesses out there, will be enough to win others over to this operating system.

But there are a few other benefits that are going to show up as well.

This operating system is going to work and keep out the troubles for as long as you choose to work with it.

And it is often able to fight off issues of ransomware and malware and even viruses better than some of the others.

And you will not need to reboot this all that often unless the kernel has to be updated, and this is often only done every few years.

If you have ever been frustrated with the operating system that you are working with and how it may not always do what you would like, that means it may be time for you to work with the Linux operating system.

It is going to have all of the benefits that we want and will also be free to use, no matter how many computers you decide to hook it up to along the way.

Open Sourced

Another thing that we are going to enjoy when it is time to work with the Linux system is that it is open-sourced.

This means that it is going to be distributed under this source license so that you can work with it in the manner that you would like.

Open source is going to be useful for a number of reasons, but we will find that there are a few key tenants that we need to focus on, include:

- You will find that you have the freedom to run the program, no matter what the purpose is.

- You will find that you have the freedom to study and learn more about how this program works and what you can make any of the changes to it that you wish along the way.

- You have the freedom to redistribute copies so that you can use it more than once for your own needs or to provide it to your neighbor who would like to use it as well.

- You will find that you have the freedom to make some modifications to it in the manner that you would like, and then you can also distribute copies of these modifications to others.

There are going to be crucial points to understand when it comes to working with the Linux system and understanding more about the community that is going to work to create this kind of platform in the first place.

Without a double, this is going to be an operating system that is by the people and for the people.

These tenants are also going to be a big factor in why people are going to choose to work with this kind of operating system compared to some of the others.

It is all about freedom, and freedom of use, and the freedom of choice, and the freedom to not have to worry about a bunch of crazy rules and other issues along the way.

Chapter 3: Installation Basics

Take note that you might need to know your computer's hardware before you install certain distributions.

For instance, if you choose to install Debian, you will need information about your PC and its components because the distribution does not recognize everything.

Fortunately, nowadays, all installers are capable of scanning your computer and see every connected hardware element.

However, you should still have the information handy in case some errors occur.

This way, you can troubleshoot and figure out what went wrong during the setup process.

Once you've selected your Linux distribution, you need to download it.

Most of them, if not all, come in ISO format, and you can download them for free.

The next step is to burn the file on a disk or a flash drive.

Next, you need to tell the system to boot up from the disk or flash drive when you start it up.

Many computers will boot automatically when they detect a boot-up disk, but sometimes you have to turn on the setting yourself if it's set to always boot from the hard drive.

This problem can be solved by changing the boot-up order.

You will have to access your system's options.

You gain access to your system by pressing a key like F10, or "DEL" before your operating system loads.

Once you're in the computer's setup section, you need to assign your Linux boot up disk to be the default boot device.

Confirm the change, place your disk in the drive (or connect the flash drive), and restart your computer.

At this stage, you should probably know whether you want to keep your current operating system at the same time as installing Linux.

If you have Windows installed, for instance, and you don't want to replace it, you will have to perform a few additional steps.

As mentioned earlier, if you plan on keeping your current operating system, the first thing you need to do is prepare a separate drive partition for the Linux distribution.

Currently, your system is using the entire hard drive.

The process isn't difficult, but there's always the risk of accidentally wiping the drive clean and losing all of your data.

This is why, before installing any operating system, it's a good idea to back-up all of your files and data.

Once you have a backup, you can use a partitioning application to make the process easier.

For instance, a program called QTParted works well, and it comes included with certain Linux distributions.

Many Linux installers can handle your partitions automatically.

The new partition is created by shrinking the size of your current operating system's partition.

Once you're ready to install Linux, boot your computer from the installation disk and begin the process.

There will be a number of steps you need to follow, and the entire setup may take up to two hours.

It all depends on your system and which distribution you're installing.

At this stage, all you really need to do is follow the onscreen instructions.

Most modern, up to date distributions guide you through an easy to follow graphical user interface.

One important element of the installation involves the hard drive partitioning.

Yes, even if you already performed the partitioning step above.

All you need to do is use the partition you already setup.

The openSUSE installation interface that comes with a number of distributions should show you the recommended steps you need to take.

Once you perform the guided configuration, which includes basic steps such as time and network setups, you need to select which packages you want to install.

Keep in mind that some Linux distributions are setup to install certain components, and you won't have the option to choose.

Once the installation process is complete, restart your computer.

This step is part of the setup process and is necessary.

Now Linux is ready to run.

When you boot up the system for the first time, you will find a few more optional steps that involve further system configuration and installing various packages and applications.

Linux Flash Drive

Using Linux Live disks is a good way to explore the large variety of distributions available to you.

You don't have to go through a time-consuming installation process, and you don't need to worry about endangering your current system to something you aren't familiar with.

This is why CDs and DVDs with Live installation were so popular at one point.

Nowadays, while you can still choose to go with disks if you want to, most people choose to go with the more modern flash drive.

Many people don't even install disk readers anymore because of the more practical USB drive, which is faster, easier to use, and can hold a lot more data.

The biggest issue with Live disks is that they are slow when it comes to reading or writing data.

Another problem is the difficulty you would encounter when it comes to operating system configuration.

It's not that easy to save certain changes to a Live disk.

That is why, in this section, we are going to focus on bootable flash drive distributions.

Bootable flash distributions have been around for years, as the technology isn't exactly new.

However, until recently, many of them came with a number of disadvantages.

One of the most popular Live distributions is probably Fedora because it's easy to prepare.

The installation is free of any risks to your system, you can maintain any other files you may have on your flash drive, and most importantly it is easy to save your Linux system configurations and modifications.

The simplest way to create a bootable Linux drive is by taking advantage of your current operating system.

It may sound strange, but performing this process using Windows is a lot easier for a beginner than typing a set of command-line instructions.

In our example, we will focus on using Windows since many people interested in Linux seem to be using this system.

However, if you are using Mac, the steps should be nearly the same.

Therefore you should be able to adapt the process on your own.

Here are the following steps you need to follow to create a bootable USB drive:

- First, you need to download the live USB-creator applications.
- Install the program by following its very straightforward setup guide.
- Locate the installation folder and run the application.
- Select the flash drive option, which you can find under the "target device."

The drive should appear along the lines of "MyDrive."

- Now you need to select where the ISO file comes from. Choose the download option to access it.

- Next, you need to choose the "persistent storage" amount.

  This represents the storage space, which will be reserved for the installation.

  Keep in mind that the application might set the default to 0MB.

  You should opt for 400MB, at least.

- Finally, you can click on the "Create Live USB" button.

  The process will take several minutes, and in the end, you will see two new folders.

  One named "syslinux," which is small and is only responsible for the system boot up.

  The second folder is "LiveOS," which contains the system and utilizes the amount of storage you set-up earlier.

  You can now terminate the flash drive creator and try out the Live drive.

Virtual Machines

VirtualBox is a virtual machine that, first developed by Sun Microsystems, is now under the ownership of Oracle.

It simulates a separate computer, and each virtual machine can have its own applications, operating system, and a whole host of other things.

VirtualBox is ideal for testing out various operating systems, in this case, Linux on a Windows or Mac OS computer.

By using Linux in this way, you don't need to make any permanent changes to your current system.

We're going to look at how to install VirtualBox on Windows and Mac

Windows

- Go to the VirtualBox Download page and find the latest version; click on it

- On the next page, look for the file that ends .exe and download it – remember the location you saved it to on your computer

- Once the installer has been downloaded, double-click on the .exe file and follow the instructions on the screen to install it onto Windows – be aware that you may lose your network connection for a while during the installation because virtual network adaptors are being installed.

- Now you must reboot your computer, and you should find VirtualBox in your apps.

From here, you can run it and install any other operating system that you want to try.

Mac OS

- Go the VirtualBox download page and download the latest version of the app for the Mac

- Save the .dmg to a file location that you will easily remember – make sure you download the OS X hosts version

- Locate the file and install it using the executable file

- Reboot your computer, and you can start using VirtualBox

Installing Linux Using an Image for VirtualBox

Windows

After you have followed the above steps to install VirtualBox to your computer, you need to download the disk image for Ubuntu Linux

- First, if you haven't already got a BitTorrent client installed on your computer, download one now – BitTorrent is a P2P application that allows downloads from other users, significantly easing the loading in the Ubuntu servers.

- Now head to the Ubuntu release website and download the latest release version – do NOT click on any links for Desktop CD.

  You will find a full list of links at the bottom of the page and make sure you click one with the .iso.torrent extension – download it to a location you will remember

- Now copy that to a bootable USB

A note of caution here – if you have got WinRAR installed, it will automatically associate itself with the file you downloaded and will ask you if you want to use WinRAR to extract the contents – do NOT use WinRAR and do NOT extract the .iso

<u>IMPORTANT – Before you start the next step back up the contents of your hard drive somewhere safe! If you don't, you will lose everything!</u>

- Open VirtualBox from your Start menu and click New – this will open the New Virtual Machine Wizard

- Click on Next and give your virtual machine a name – stick with Ubuntu or Linux for ease

- If you have more than 1 GB of RAM on your computer, allocate one-quarter maximum to the virtual machine – if you have less, stick with what VirtualBox recommends. Click Next

- Click on Create New Hard Disk and then on Next

- Click on Next again, and you will come to a screen where you set the type of hard drive. Choose Fixed-Size Storage

- If you intend to add software or to install potentially large files in virtual Linux, add on some buffer; click Create

- Once the virtual hard drive has been created, you need to add the .iso image you downloaded. Click Settings>Storage>CD/DVD Device

- Where it says Empty, there is a folder icon so click on it

- Choose the .iso that you already downloaded and click on OK

- Now double-click on the virtual machine, so it starts

- You will more than likely get a load of instructions and warnings about using guest operating systems – read and then mark them, so they don't come up again.

- Wait while Ubuntu loads

- Before you can install Linux, you must first change your BIOS settings on your computer – usually, when you start your computer, you hit F1, F2, F12, Escape or Delete.

  Restart your computer now and get into the BIOS settings and change the boot option to boot from USB first

- Now plug your USB stick in and reboot your computer again

- You will see a screen that is blank except for a few logos at the bottom

- Press any key, and a new screen will appear – choose the language you want

- Now click on Install Ubuntu

- The installer will start, and you may be asked to choose your language again

- Tick the option for installing closed source software

- Now you will be asked to connect to your Wi-Fi if you aren't connected already – you don't need to do this right now, and it will make your installation take longer so ignore it

- There are three options here – choose the first one and then drag the slider to choose the hard drive sizes for Windows and for Ubuntu.

  Your hard drive will now be partitioned

- Answer the questions that appear on your screen as they appear – these are self-explanatory

- Now you just wait for Ubuntu to be installed – depending on the speed of your computer this can take up to one hour

- Reboot your computer and remove your USB stick – when you boot up again you will be in a working Ubuntu environment

If you changed the size of your partition for Windows, you would be asked to do a disk check – this is not necessary.

Go back to Settings>Storage>CD/DVD and check that it has the Empty entry again – this will eliminate the need to use your USB every time you boot your computer.

Mac OS

When the VirtualBox installation has completed, you need to download the iso

- Go to the Ubuntu download page and click on the Mac iso image – choose your geographical location and then click on Begin Download.

  Make sure you save the file and not open or mount it

- Open VirtualBox and register it

- Now you can create a new virtual machine – click on New to open the wizard

- Click Next and type in a name for the virtual machine

- Choose Linux Ubuntu from the operating system menu and click on Next

- Set your base memory as 384 MB and click on Next

- Now you need to click to create a new hard disk, which is just a disk that takes up space on your existing drive – make sure you have enough to do this!

  Accept all the default settings and click on Next

- The Create New Virtual Disk Wizard will appear, click on Next

- Click on Dynamically Expanding Storage and click on Next

- Choose where you want your hard drive to be and how big – 2 TB is the maximum although 8 GB is more than sufficient

- Click on Next and then on Finish

- The framework is ready so make sure you have copied the iso to a bootable USB or DVD disk

VirtualBox will now show you that you have a virtual machine with the name of Ubuntu Linux.

- Insert your DVD or USB

- Click on CD/DVD and then tick the box for Mount CD/DVD drive

- Click on ISO Image File

- Click the folder beside No Media and then drag your iso file into it

- Click on Select and then on OK

- Click on Start, and a black screen will appear – this is the new session and everything you do now will be done on the virtual machine – if you want to change that back to your Mac just press the Command key on the left side of the space bar

- Click OK

- When the Ubuntu screen appears, double click on Install and answer the questions that appear on the screen

- When finished click on Forward

- Now accept the default values for where Ubuntu is going and click on Forward

- Input your personal information, including a new password and a name for your machine

- Choose whether to log in automatically or use a password and click on Forward

- Click Install and wait

- When the installation has finished, you will either be asked to use your password to go in, or you will automatically be at the Linux desktop, depending on what option you chose

- Ubuntu will now check for updates so click on Install Updates and wait

- Reboot your Mac is needed, and you are ready to go

Steps of Installing CentOS from Scratch

CentOS is a stable Linux distribution and here's how to install it:

- Go to the download page for CentOS and download the ISO

- Now you need to make up a bootable drive, transferring the ISO to a formatted USB stick.

  To do this, plug your USB in and open a command prompt window.

  Type the following in - # dd if=/iso/CentOS-versionnumber-x86_64-DVD-1602-99.iso of=/dev/sdb – ensure that you have a minimum 5 GB space on the USB stick

- On the desktop, click on Install to Hard Drive

- Choose your keyboard type and preferred language – make sure you pick the right keyboard or some of your keys will be scrambled up

- The default for the installer is to select Automatic Partitioning of your hard drive – click the icon for Installation Destination and change by selecting Custom Partitioning

- Choose your hard drive where the installation of CentOS is to be stored and then click on Other Storage Options

- Select the option giving you a chance to configure the partitioning by yourself and then click on Done

- Select the Standard Partition

- To come up with a Swap Space on one of your partitions, select File System where the swap space will be created and name it as swap.

  Select Reformat

- Now you need to create your mount point –where to install root partition.

  Set your mount point and then set Label and Desired Capacity in any way you desire.

- Click on ext4 to set file system and then on Reformat

- Click Done and accept the changes you have made

- Click the clock and set your time zone; click Done

- Click on Begin Installation; as it goes through, follow all the onscreen instructions, setting up your user account and the root password.

To do this, click Root Password and type in the password twice; click on Done

- To create your user account, input the details and, if this is going to be an administrator account, ensure that you tick the options for Make This User Administrator and on Require a Password

- Once the installation is complete, you will see a message telling you it was successful; click on Quit

- Log out and then log in to your new CentOS installation

- Accept the EULA, and you are ready to go

Connecting Your Linux System over the Network

If you are looking to connect your Linux system over your network, you must use something like SSH.

This is an acronym for Secure Shell, and it is one of the most well-known of the network protocols.

The purpose of SSH is to let you connect securely to remote machines on your network.

To connect your Linux system over your network:

- **Windows** – use PuTTY

- **Mac and Linux** – use ssh on the command line

Windows

- Open your web browser and download PuTTY

- Open PuTTY and type in the IP address or Hostname into the correct box.

- If you had no port number provided, leave it as the default of 22

- Click on Data and then on the Auto-Login Username – input your username

- To save a session, click the Saved Sessions box, type in a name and click on

    Save in the future you will be able to double click the saved session to connect

- Click on Open, and a connection is made.

    When you connect to a server for the first time, PuTTY will ask for permission to cache the host key for the server – click on Yes

Linux and Mac

Both Linux and Mac already have the SSH client built-in as a command-line program. To get to it run the terminal:

- **Mac** – Applications folder

- **Linux** – Open Dashboard and search for Terminal

When the terminal has been started, simply use the ssh command to get your connection.

Do be aware that commands are always case-sensitive, so only use lowercase.

Type in ssh followed by the username on the Linux server

When you connect for the first time to a server, you will need to verify the host key.

Type Yes to continue connecting and then press Enter.

When the connection is established, input your password.

To get out of the connection, type in exit and then log out

Chapter 4: Linux Distributions

A Linux distribution or a "distro" is a complete Linux package consisting of the kernel and other components.

There are many distributors who integrate and distribute these so that end-users do not have to do anything complex.

Linux distributions consist of the operating system itself and a number of certain applications and libraries, all packed into one single installation file.

For instance, there's a number of scientific distributions used by data scientists, analysts, and machine learners.

They come with the OS and the tools and libraries which they need to work on their projects.

Why choose a distribution instead of the standard installation? Simply because of convenience.

Taking the scientific distribution example above, without it, a data scientist would have to install a number of applications, as well as download and import the libraries they need one at a time.

This process can be extremely time consuming, and it is highly unnecessary.

There are 288 Linux distributions currently and are gradually declining.

Peaked at 323, and now it is 288.

These distributions are specific or targeting a specific user group, or a functional group, such as developers, infrastructure, multimedia, or even general users. Let's look at three major types of distributions.

- Core distributions.
- Special distributions.
- Live CDs.

Most applications are customized for desktop users and business users.

It includes facilities to install and use Linux easier, popular operating system-like desktop distributions (e.g., similar to Windows or Mac), and autodetection/configuration of hardware.

These distributions made Linux revolutionary popular among desktop users.

Major Linux Distributions

Slackware Patrick Volkerding created Slackware during 1992 and is the oldest surviving Linux distro.

It is famous for the bug-free and clean distributions.

It runs on both 32-bit (i486) and 64-bit (x86_64) architectures.

The philosophy is similar to Arch Linux.

There are few drawbacks, such as the limited number of application support and upgrade complexities.

Debian GNU/Linux came to existence in 1993.

Today Debian can be thought of as the largest Linux distro and largest possible collaborative software project.

According to Distrowatch, Debian is developed by more than 1000 volunteers, 50000+ binary packages, and inspiring over 120 distros.

Debian is highly stable, has outstanding quality assurance, and supports the most processor architectures in contrast to others.

One of the main drawbacks is the release of stable updates (2-3 years).

Fedora

Fedora is one of the most innovative Linux distros at present.

It is linked to the famous Red Hat Linux.

In 2003, Red Hat introduced a revolutionary change: the Fedora Core.

It is introduced as a community edition designed for Linux hobbyists.

Right now, Red Hat is the most profitable enterprise.

Fedora presents outstanding security, supports multiple desktop environments, contributed to the kernel advancements, Glibc and GCC, SELinux integration, journaled file system, system, and other enterprise features.

It also supports both 32-bit and 64-bit environments.

It is geared toward more enterprise features and users.

Red Hat and CentOS

Red Hat holds the flagship in the enterprise.

It started in 1995.

It had many innovative components, such as Anaconda GIU-based installer, RPM package manager, and more.

Regrettably, it failed to maintain its phase with rising patent issues and similar.

It ended its life in 2003 and gave birth to RHEL (Red Hat Enterprise Linux) and Fedora core.

RHEL is undoubtedly the industry de-facto.

It can operate on platforms like x86_64, Arm64, Power ISA, IBM Z, and desktop platforms.

It has huge variations targeting different enterprise-class applications such as servers and workstations.

In the meantime, Fedora works as the upstream for future RHEL versions.

Given the leadership and influence, exceptional support, cutting edge technology, RHEL is superb for enterprise use.

It is used by tech giants.

Gentoo

Gentoo is a highly flexible meta distribution that allows users to run a verity of kernels and software configurations.

Gentoo can be customized.

This project was introduced by Daniel Robbins in 2000.

Even though it offers flexibility, it requires expertise to use.

In other words, this is not suitable for inexperienced users, as it may take more time to get used to it.

The upgrades can be time-consuming.

Arch Linux

Arch Linux was launched by Judd Vinet in 2002.

In the beginning, it was considered as a marginal project

that existed between intermediate and advanced users.

Later on, it was promoted using a feature called "rolling- release."

Rolling-release means the operating system has the ability to keeps itself up to date.

Arch Linux has an excellent software management infrastructure.

It is included the ability to install software from the source code.

One of the disadvantages is the risk of breakdown due to occasional instabilities.

Ubuntu

Ubuntu revolutionizes Linux for desktop users.

It has been popular for a long time.

It was launched in 2004 and is still popular among Linux users.

Ubuntu is based on DEB packages.

It has long-term support via Canonical, and it even supports the enterprise now with its server edition.

Some special features of Ubuntu are that it includes an installable live DVD, it supports new technologies where a novice can easily get used to Ubuntu and the different desktop environments.

One of the Significant disadvantages of Ubuntu is its lack of compatibility.

MX Linux

MX Linux was introduced as a replacement for MEPIS Linux.

This was designed for personal purposes as well as business.

The most popular feature of MX Linux is its graphical

administrative tools, known as MX-Tools.

It also has exceptional support for the platform, exceptional compatibility with graphics drivers, and the ease of administration.

MX Linux may not be friendly for novices when compared to Mint and Ubuntu.

It takes time to get used to it, and its installer and some tools may appear different.

Mint

Linux Mint was launched in 2006.

It was designed based on Ubuntu.

This distribution is the best for beginners. Mint has a wide range of enhancements that make it user-friendly.

It provides interoperability with other operating systems.

Therefore, it is suitable not only for personal use but also for the enterprise.

The developers offer three types of releases namely official (in December), point releases (as needed, e.g., bug fixes) and a monthly snapshot release.

This makes Mint highly stable.

Backtrack and Kali

There are other special Linux editions geared toward system security and penetration.

Kali Linux is the most popular penetration testing platform at present.

It all started with the creation of BackTrack from the merger of WHAX (WHAX was a Slax based Linux distribution.

The company that was behind this was **Offensive Security**.

Earlier versions of WHAX was based on Knoppix and named Whoppix).

BackTrack 5 was based on Ubuntu Lucid LTS.

It supported both 32-bit and 64-bit architectures and ARM.

In 2013, the company rebuilt the platform based on Debian and released in under the name Kali.

Kali Linux is highly stable and advanced with its capabilities and the set of top-level penetration testing tools.

What about Android?

Android is the largest distribution based on a modified version of the Linux kernel, and Google's own libraries.

Android also runs a virtual platform called Dalvin to run the applications written in Java.

Such applications target different hardware platforms, and it depends on Google APIs.

You cannot run a desktop version of Linux in an Android device.

You cannot run a mobile Android version in a PC (without emulation and virtualization).

Linux Live CDs

Linux Live CDs and USBs are quite popular among a variety of users.

It goes beyond simply learning what Linux is before the installation.

Many Linux live distributions support running an operating system from a CD ROM.

It is great for demonstration purposes and to test out things.

The customized distributions include packages to carry out various simple and complex system tasks, such as changing hard disk layouts, security and recovery procedures, and many more.

These versions are now appearing as Linux Live USB distributions.

All the major distributions support live CD functionality.

Linux Live CD Distributions

Puppy Linux

Puppy Linux is a small system that is less than 200MB.

This Linux distribution is best for basic computer functions and web browsing.

Even though it is ultra-small, file recovery tools and partitioning are still available.

This distribution makes it easy to install other popular applications because it has its own package manager.

Puppy Linux has various customized versions known as "puplets."

One of the advantages of the Puppy Linux is it can be used in older hardware.

Slax

Slax is a small and fast Linux distribution.

It was based on Slackware.

But now it's based on Debian stable.

It is one of the user-friendly Linux distribution.

Users can delete or add modules when downloading.

Slax is quite convenient.

This distribution can be booted by different media such as USB flash or DVD ROM.

Slax has a boot menu that includes many options.

Knoppix Knoppix Is a stable Linux distribution.

It is one of the very first Linux CDs.

This is well established and has over 1000 software packages.

One of the advantages of Knoppix is, it supports distinctive hardware.

Even though Knoppix is aimed to run from live media, it can also be installed into a hard drive.

There are many derivatives of Knoppix.

Tiny Core Linux Tiny Core Linux distribution is a very small portable operating system.

It is only 10MB. Since this operating system is very small, it does not include applications or a file manager.

However, users can install them later.

This is one of the recommended options for beginners.

Ubuntu Ubuntu does not have a specific LiveCD.

However, its ISO image can be burned onto a DVD or set up into a USB as bootable.

It has an option to try upon booting from it.

MX Linux MX Linux is suitable for both older and modern computers.

This is a user-friendly distribution, and novice can use this.

Chapter 5: GNU Utilities

In this chapter, we will cover the general components of the Linux operating system.

We will delve into the critical elements that work together to make Linux the most versatile operating system.

You will understand the difference between the GNU project and the GPL.

All Linux distributions come with software developed under the GNU project.

When you use the distro in text terminal mode, you will be able to see the GNU utilities.

What is GNU?

GNU (GNU's Not Unix) is a free operating system of GNU packages that were released under the GNU project and other third parties free software.

Linux has become the most preferred operating system recently because it comes with all the software installed.

Linux distributions come with graphics software, office packages, and even coding packages under the GNU GPL license.

In 1984, Richard Stallman started the GNU project, which was intended to be a UNIX based Operating system.

GNU utilities are a collection of GNU software that contains tools like Is, Cat, and rm, which are mostly implemented in Unix Operating systems.

rm – is a command used to remove objects like computer files, directories, and links from file systems.

cat – is a Unix utility that reads files in sequence and writes them as standard output. Name derived from its functionality; to con**cat**enate.

ls – is the command used to list files in Unix System and all UNIX based systems.

The GNU General Public License (GPL) for Linux, ensures that the software is always free and open to anyone.

No single person or/and a company can claim ownership or control its use.

Additionally, any user can copy, edit, and re-distribute the software's source code.

You may ask yourself, then who funds the GNU project?

How do they raise funds?

The Free Software Foundation funds the project (FSF), a tax-exempted charity organization.

The GNOME GUI and the bash are both programs made under the GNU project.

The ***Shell*** is the GNU program that executes your commands, most commonly referred to as the command interpreter.

Linux distributions are developed using GNU C and C++ compiler.

Text files in Linux are edited using the **ed** and **emacs** editors.

- ***Example of GNU Utilities***

Other popular GNU utilities include:

- **Binutils -** is comprised of different packages for handling binary files.

  Accompanying packages include ar, as, gasp, id, nm, objcopy, objdump, ranlib, readlf, size, and strip.

- **Bash** – is the GNU package responsible for interpreting shell commands in Linux.

- **Automake** – is the GNU software for generating a makefile.in files that are used with Autoconf.

- **Autoconf** – is the package for generating shell scripts that are used for configuring source-code packages.

- **Emacs** – is the text editor package for Linux.

- **Ed** – is the line-oriented text editor.

- **Diff** – is the package used to compare files and show the difference line by line.

- **GNU Chess** – is the package for running the Linux chess game.

- **The GIMP** – is a GNU program for manipulating images. It's like photoshop for Linux.

- **GNOME** – provides the display or GUI for Linux Distributions.

- **Gnumeric** – is a spreadsheet GNU program that works on GNOME GUIs. It's an equivalent of MS. Excel.

- **Time** – is a GNU program that manages time for the user.

Chapter 6: The Shell

Before the development of graphical user interfaces, users interacted with the computer system by typing commands in a terminal.

UNIX systems, which are the foundation of Linux, used what is known as a shell to interpret the instructions.

The shell is still available, and some users prefer it over the GUI, while others only use it for specific tasks.

Keep in mind that it doesn't matter which Linux distribution you installed.

The shell is available to all of them.

The Linux shell allows writing scripts that can be executed to run various programs, compile code, manage the operating system, and perform nearly every operation you can imagine.

While the shell isn't as user-friendly as a GUI, especially to beginners used to Windows or Mac, many developers and Linux experts consider it superior.

One of the reasons, as stated earlier, is the fact that some of the more complex features offered by Linux cannot be accessed or manipulated through any other means except shell commands.

In this section, we are going to focus on the "bash" shell, which stands for Bourne Again Shell because it's one of the most common ones you are likely to encounter.

There are a few other shells on different distributions.

However, they are essentially no different than bash.

Most other shells are used in UNIX distributions.

However, Ubuntu uses the dash shell, which is, in fact, an improved version of bash.

While it's very likely for your distribution to have bash pre-installed, it probably has other shells as well.

However, it's recommended for you to stick to what is considered the standard, especially as a beginner.

Even if you are using Ubuntu, which comes with the dash, you can install bash on it without a problem.

With that being said, here are a few real-world examples of why learning how to use the Linux shell is a vital step on your journey to master this operating system:

- If you know how to work through the shell, you will be able to control any Linux or Unix system available on the market.

  For instance, you will be able to connect to your Red Hat Linux web server, your home entertainment server, router, and even your home computer from the shell. All of this can be achieved remotely and at the same time.

You can even use your Android smartphone to issue the commands because all of these devices and technologies run a form of Linux or Unix.

- A large number of expert Linux users work exclusively with the shell because they learned it could be more powerful, efficient, and even faster than any GUI.

For instance, you can even avoid a great deal of typing and issue lightning-fast commands by finding and using commands from the shell's command history.

- You might be thinking that there is no way you can issue complex commands fast enough.

Even if you find and edit the history commands, you still need time to create sequences of commands.

Luckily, you can create your own programs that contain a number of complex commands that take too long to type.

You can gather these commands and apply them through conditional statements, loops, and case statements.

This way, you can nearly eliminate typing and perform a difficult operation at the touch of a button.

This is called shell scripting, and it is very popular among system administrators who want to automate most of their tasks.

For instance, with the proper script, the system can perform regular system backups, monitor various files, and verify the integrity and security of the system.

The shell is essentially a command language interpreter.

If you are familiar with Windows operating systems, you may notice that the shell is similar to the interpreter, which manages commands in DOS.

It is also similar to the CMD interface.

However, it is far more powerful and versatile.

You might dislike using the shell at first because you are used to a GUI, and you will feel that typing commands is slow.

Later, you will have to rely on it at the very least to manage certain advanced features or fix a system problem.

The Shell Prompt

If your Linux distribution didn't come with a GUI, or it wasn't configured probably, you probably used the shell prompt to log into your system after booting.

It's important to take note that there are two different prompts depending on the type of your account.

If you are connected to your system as a regular user, then the prompt is displayed as a dollar sign "$."

If you are logged in as the root user (the equivalent of administrator user in Windows), the prompt appears as a hash sign "#."

Depending on your Linux distribution, both prompts are usually preceded by the username, system name, and the current directory (the equivalent of a Windows folder).

For instance, let's say we have a login prompt for a user called Steve and a system called flynet and you are currently navigating the /usr/share/ directory.

It would look something like this:

[steve@flynet share]$

The prompt can be customized and modified to show anything you want, including information about your system.

For instance, you can set up a sequence of characters or display the computer's name, the date, and the directory you're in.

There are many features at your disposal when using the shell, and the easiest way to start exploring them is by typing commands.

The best way to become accustomed to the command interface is through practice.

Just keep in mind that certain commands can only be issued while logged in as the root user.

You need administrative access to the system to use some of the tools.

The command you issue appears after the prompt, and once you hit the "enter" button, you will see one or several lines that display the result of your instruction.

Running Commands

The most basic commands you can type are the ones that are most obvious.

Open the terminal and type the following line:

$ date

This simple instruction is self-explanatory.

It will display the current date and time recorded by your computer system.

Keep in mind that if you do not specify any parameters or arguments, you will only receive the most basic default output.

Here's another example with several commands issued back to back:

$ pwd

/home/john

$ hostname

mycomputer

$ ls

DesktopDownloadsPicturesTemplates

DocumentsMusicPublicVideos

The first command, "pwd," displays the directory you are currently in.

Next, by typing the "hostname" command, you instruct the computer to tell you its hostname.

Finally, the "ls" commands stand for list, and it does just that.

It lists all of the directories that the current directory contains.

These commands are basic one-word instructions.

Normally you wouldn't issue such simple commands.

Instead, you would add more information in the form of arguments in order to obtain a more specific output.

Everything you type after the command itself is referred to as options and arguments.

Syntax

You can attach options to most commands in order to manipulate their behavior.

They are represented by a single, hyphenated letter.

Keep in mind that you can group up a number of options or arguments.

There is no real limit, as long as the command makes sense.

Here are a couple of examples:

ls -l -a -t

ls -lat

Notice the fact that both commands are the same.

One contains options that are separated from each other with a hyphen, while the other groups them together with only one hyphen to precede the group.

In both examples, we have the "ls" command, which is further detailed with the long listing command "-l," show hidden files "a," and the list by time command "-t."

Certain options aren't necessarily written as one letter.

They sometimes come as entire words.

The best example is the help option "--help."

In order to use a whole word, we need double hyphens.

Why?

Because if we used one hyphen, the shell would interpret the command as a group of one letter instructions, like the example above.

An option such as --help works with a large number of commands like this:

date --help

In addition to options, you can also attach arguments to a command.

They are entered after the options or at the end of the line.

Arguments are additional bits of data.

This includes directory names, devices, username and anything else which explicitly instructs the command itself to act on something specific.

Here's an example:

cat /etc/passwd

The cat command is told to display the information contained in the passwd file, which is located in the etc directory.

The specific instruction is an argument. Keep in mind that just like with options, you can have as many arguments without nearly any limit.

In some cases, however, an argument works only with specific options.

This is an exception which calls for the argument after the option.

If the option is the single letter type, then the argument is separated from it by one space.

If the options are an entire word, then the equal sign is used to act as a separator.

Here's an example:

$ ls --hide=Desktop

This is the whole word option, and you will notice that there are no spaces between the option and the argument.

The command itself tells the system to list the contents of the directory you are in, just as we did earlier.

However, we use the "hide" option with the "Desktop" argument to instruct the system to hide the desktop directory from the listing process.

Now, let's take a look at an example with one letter options:

tar -cvf mybackup.tar /home/john

Here we create a backup file called "mybackup.tar."

The backup will contain every single file inside the john directory.

Chapter 7: Basic Functions of Linux

Now it's time to move on to some of the basics that you are going to need to learn in order to use Linux confidently.

These functions are important for helping you to navigate the computer system with ease.

Let's take a bit of time now to look at these basic functions, and learn how they can work for us.

Logging In and Out of the Interface

When it comes to the Linux operating system, you are first going to need to provide your login credentials, meaning username and password, each time that you try to get onto the system.

In addition to this, there are two modes that you can choose between when you are running the Linux system, and we will take a look at them below:

Graphical Mode

The graphical mode is going to be the default mode for your desktop computer.

Basically, if the computer screen is asking for the password and username before letting you on, you will know that you are using the graphical mode.

To sign in, you will just need to enter in the login credentials that you have already set up, and then hit OK or ENTER to continue.

After you enter this login information, it can sometimes take a few minutes to get everything loaded up and ready to go; the amount of time that it takes for things to get going will depend on how powerful your computer is and its processing capabilities.

When the computer has finished loading, you will need to open up an 'xterm', otherwise known as a terminal window.

You will be able to find this tool by simply clicking on Applications and then choosing Utilities.

Note: in some of the newer versions of Linux, there will be an icon available to speed up this process, and you can just click on that rather than going through the steps above.

The terminal window is basically going to be the control panel for your operating system.

Most of the procedures that you want to do with the operating system can be done with this tool, and as a general rule, when you open the terminal window, it should display some kind of command prompt.

Usually, this is going to start out with your username for the system, as well as some information about updates that were performed.

When you are ready to log out with this mode, you need to make sure that you have closed out of the terminal windows and all of the open programs.

You can then find the icon for logging out or search for the Log Out option on your main menu.

If you forget to close out of an application or a window, it isn't that big of a deal since the computer can do it for you, but the system is going to try and retrieve all of these windows and programs the next time you come back, and this can slow down the process of getting your computer started.

Once you see that the screen is once again asking for your login credentials, you will then know that you are all logged out of the system.

Text Mode

The other mode that you can use for your credentials on this system is the text mode.

You will be able to see that you are in text mode when the whole screen is black with just a few characters on it.

This mode's screen is going to show a bit of data, including the name of the computer, a bit of data about that computer, and then a prompt that is usable for signing in.

This one is going to be a bit different compared to the graphical mode because you will need to press the ENTER key once you are done typing in the username, as there is not going to be a clickable button or link on the screen.

You can then type in the password and hit ENTER once again.

A nice thing about this mode is that while you are typing in the username and password, you will not see any signs that you are typing.

You won't see the words, letters, or even dots and special characters come up while you are typing.

This can be confusing to some people who are brand new to using this system, but it operates this way for security purposes.

Once the system accepts your username and password, you will receive the message of the day.

Some of the distributions of Linux will have a feature that is known as the fortune cookie feature, and that is going to provide you with some extra thoughts each day.

Then, the system will move on to providing you with a shell, explained with the same details that you would get when using the graphical mode.

When you are ready to log out from this system, you will simply need to type in 'logout' and then press ENTER.

You will be able to tell that you are logged out from the system successfully when the screen comes back up and asks you for your login credentials again.

The Basic Commands

Now that we understand how to log in and out of the Linux system based on the type of mode we are in, it is time to start working on some of the basic commands that we will be using.

These are pretty simple to learn, and if you have worked with some programming languages in the past, you may have seen some of these commands before.

Some of the commands that you should learn as a beginner include:

- Is - this is going to show a set of files that are in the directory that you are using at this point in time.
- Passwd - this command is going to change the password of the user who is currently on the system.
- Pwd - this is going to show the current working directory.
- Cd directory - this is going to change the directories.

- Exit or log out - this is going to make it easier to leave the current session.
- Info command - this is going to read info pages on command.
- File 'filename'- this is going to show the file type of the file that is given a certain name.
- Apropos string - this one will search for strings using the 'what is' database.
- cat: This command can be used to print the content of a file to your screen.

  It is great for exploring a file when you quickly need some information, or you want to see what data it contains because you don't need first to open a text editor or word processor.

- cp: This command will copy a file or folder.

  Keep in mind you will have also to specify where to place the copy.

- mv: This is the move command, which moves directories and files.

  It can also be used to rename files like this: mv old_filename new_filename.

- mkdir: Creates a new directory.
- rmdir: Removes a directory.

- sudo: This is an important command; however, it can be risky using it.

    You learned earlier that there are certain features that can only be accessed with the root account.

    This means that you have to relog from your regular user account to the root account before you can perform a restricted operation.

    The sudo command provides you with a shortcut.

    By typing this command in front of another command, you tell the system that you have administrative power, and you want to proceed without switching accounts.

- locate: A useful command used to locate a file or directory.

    Use it as a search button.

    Keep in mind that you will first have to update the system's database to make sure it recorded every file and directory.

    You can do this with the following command: sudo updated.

    Now you will be able to perform the search.

Access, you may want to use the -i option along with the command in order to ignore upper or lower case letters.

Here's an example: locate -i *myfile*.

- history: This command will print a list of the commands you used previously.

  Use this to learn what you did wrong.

  A shortcut to this would be pressing the Ctrl + R buttons.

- man: This is a particularly useful command for beginners.

  It is used to learn more about other commands.

  Every command line has a "man" page of its own, which explains everything it does.

  It also includes a number of options and arguments that can be used with the command.

  Here's how to use it: man insert_command.

There are many other commands, but for now, you should stick to the basics.

There's no need to overwhelm yourself. P

ractice with these commands for a while, and when you think you are ready to explore more of them, you can search the rest on your own.

Other Things to Note

In most cases, you are going to issue the commands by themselves.

For example, you can just type in "ls," and the system will be able to do the rest of the work for you.

A command is going to behave in a different manner if you specify an option, and you can do this by introducing a dash.

When working in GNU, it will accept some longer options, as long as you introduce them with two dashes, but there are some commands that won't have these extra options.

What is known as an 'argument' to a command is a specification for the object on which you want to apply the command.

A good example of this is ls / etc. for this example, the /etc would be the directory and the argument, while ls would be the command.

This particular argument is going to show that you would like to see the contents of the /etc directory rather than the default directory.

You will then be able to click on the ENTER key and go to that directory.

Depending on what you are trying to do, some of your commands will need arguments to help the system make sense of what you are looking for.

Using the Bash Features

The Bash, which is the default GNU shell on most of the Linux systems that you will use, is going to make it easier to use certain combinations of keys in order to perform a task easily and quickly.

Some of the most common features to use with the Bash shell include:

- Tab – this is going to complete the command or the filename.

If there is more than one option, the system will use a visual or audio notification to tell you.

If the system detects that there are a lot of possibilities, it will ask you whether you would like to check all of them.

- Tab Tab – this one is going to show the completion possibilities for a filename or command.

- Ctrl + A – this one is going to move the cursor over to the start of the current command line.

- Ctrl + C – this one is going to end your computer program, and then will show the Linux prompt.

- Ctrl + D – this one is going to log you out of your current session.

It is the same as logout or exit.

- Ctrl + E – moves your cursor towards the end of your current command line.

- Ctrl + H – this is going to work similarly to pressing the backspace key on the keyboard.

- Ctrl + L – this one is going to clear out the current terminal.

- Ctrl + R – this is going to search through the history of commands

- Ctrl + Z – this is going to allow you to suspend your computer programs.

- Arrow right / arrow left – these keys are going to make it easier to move the cursor along the command line that you are currently on.

You may find it useful if you need to add in more characters or make some changes in the program.

- Arrow up / arrow down – these are the keys that will make it easier to browse the history of the system.

You can access any lines that you want to repeat, change some of the data when needed, and then press ENTER to execute these new commands quickly.

- Shift + Page Up/ Shift + Page Down – using these key combinations will allow you to check the terminal buffer.

As you get a bit more familiar with the Linux system, you will begin to understand better how these commands work, as well as some, learn other commands, which will make it easier to use the Linux system.

These are just a few of the initial commands that you should learn how to use because they are going to make navigating through the system much easier for you.

Give them a try and practice logging in and out of your system so that you can get a feel for how it works before moving on.

Chapter 8: Overview of Processes

If you wish to do some really neat things with Linux and make the program really work the way that you want, it is important to understand how processes work inside of this operating system.

Managing the processes

As a beginner, you may be a bit confused on how you should be managing your processes and getting them to work together, or at least getting them to work at the times when you want them to.

Here we will look at some of the steps that you should take in order to manage the different processes that are with your Linux system.

The tasks of the admin

The admin should be the person who is in charge of running the network for the rest of the computers if more than one is on the same Linux system.

That being said, if you are the only person using that part of Linux, you would technically be the admin, and this makes it important to know how to manage some of the processes within your system.

This can be important knowledge to know when you are keeping track of the efficiency of the system and getting it to work right for you.

How much time does this process require?

When you are using the Bash shell, you are going to notice that commands are going to come pre-installed on the computer.

This is going to show the amount of time that it should take to execute a process.

This tool is really helpful because it has a lot of versatility as well as accuracy, and it can be used to get the precise data that you need about any command.

You can use this to see how long it would take to complete any of the processes on your list, whether you are trying to write out some code, save a pdf file, or do something else. As you can guess, all of the different processes that you would want to do will take a different amount of time to complete.

Performance

When you think about the performance of your system, you usually want it to be quick and work well.

You want it to execute through the processes well so that you can work without delays.

For those who are system managers, though, these words have a bit more meaning because the admin needs to make sure that the performance for the whole system, including the users, programs, and daemons, is all working as well as possible.

In general, there are a few things that can affect the performance including:

- Access to interfaces, controllers, displays, and drives.
- The program that is being executed was either designed poorly, or it doesn't use the computer's resources as effectively as it should.
- How accessible the remote networks are.
- The time of day
- How many users are active on the system at the time.

When some of these are not working properly, you are going to find that the performance is going to fall a bit.

For example, if there are too many users on the system at once, it may slow down.

If a program or process that you want to use doesn't configure right within the computer system, it is going to have trouble working, and so on.

It is up to the administrator to take a look at these different aspects regularly to ensure that the computer system, as well as Linux, are able to work the whole time properly.

Priority

Linux has what is known as a 'niceness number.'

This is a number on the scale of -20 to 19.

The lower the number, the more priority that task is given, and vice versa.

If a task is number 19, for example, it will be seen as a very low priority, and the CPU will process it only when it gets a chance and other higher priority tasks have been completed.

The default nice value for a task is 0.

How important a task is will help to determine whether it is going to work well on the system.

Tasks that have a high 'nice' number are cooperative with other tasks, the network, and other users, and will be considered low priority tasks.

It is possible to make a task a bit nicer by manually changing the nice number.

Remember that this is only going to be effective for any process that will need a lot of CPU time.

Processes that are using a lot of I/O time often will be provided a low nice number, or a higher priority, so that they can get through the mess.

For example, the inputs from your keyboard are often going to receive a higher priority in the computer so that the system can register what you are trying to do.

Chapter 9: The Linux Processes

In this chapter, we will learn how to monitor and manage processes that run on Red Hat Enterprise Linux 7.

By the end of this chapter, we will be able to list processes and interpret basic information about them on the system, use bash job control to control processes, use signals to terminate processes, and monitor system resources and system load caused by processes.

- **Processes**

In this section, we will define the cycle of a typical process and understand the different states of a process. We will also learn to view and interpret processes.

- ***What is a process?***

An executable program in a state where it is running after being launched is called a process.

A process has the following features.

- Allocated memory that points to an address space
- Properties with respect to security, which include ownership privileges and credentials

- Program code that contains one or more executable threads

- The state of the process

The process environment has the following features

- Variables that are both local and global in nature

- A current scheduling context

- System resources allocated to it, which include network ports and file descriptors

An existing process is known as a parent process, which splits and duplicates its address space to create a child process.

For security and tracking, a unique process ID known as PID is assigned to every new process.

The PID and the parent process's ID, known as PPID, together, make the environment for the child process.

A child process can be created by any process.

All the processes in the system descend from the very first process of the system, which is known as **systemd** on Red Hat Enterprise Linux 7.

As the child process splits from a parent process through a fork, properties such as previous and current file descriptors, security identities, port privileges, resource privileges, program code, environment variables are all inherited by the child process.

Once these properties have been inherited, the child process can then execute its own program code.

When a child process runs, the parent process goes to sleep by setting a request to a wait flag until the child process completes.

Once the child process completes, it leaves the system and releases all system resources and environment it has previously locked, and what remains of it is known as a zombie.

Once the child process leaves, the parent process wakes up again and clean the remaining bit and starts to run its own program code again.

- **Process States**

Consider an operating system, which is capable of multitasking.

If it has hardware with a CPU that has multiple cores, every core can be dedicated to one process at a given point in time.

During runtime, the requirements of CPU and other resources keep changing for a given process.

This leads to processes being in a state, which changes as per the requirements of the current circumstance.

Let us go through the states of a process one by one by looking at the table given below.

Name	Flag	State name and description
Running	R	TASK_RUNNING: The process is waiting or executing on the CPU. The process could be executing routines for the user or the kernel. It could also be in a queued state where it is getting ready to run known as the Running state.
Sleeping	S	TASK_INTERRUPTIBLE: The process is waiting for a condition such as system resources access, hardware request, or a signal. When the condition is met by an event or signal, the process will get back to Running.
	D	TASK_UNINTERRUPTIBLE: The process is in the Sleeping state here as well, but unlike **S**, in this, it will not respond to any signals. It is used only in specific conditions where an unpredictable device state can be caused due to process interruption.

	K	TASK_KILLABLE: It is much like the uninterruptible **D** state, but the task that is waiting can respond to a signal to be killed. Killable processes are displayed as the **D** state by utilities.	
Stopped	T	TASK_STOPPED: The process is in a Stopped state because of another signal or process. Another signal can, however, send the process back into the Running state.	
	T	TASK_TRACED: A process is in a state of being debugged and is, therefore, in a Stopped state. It shares the same **T** flag.	
	Zombie	Z	EXIT_ZOMBIE: A child process is complete, and it leaves the system and lets the parent process know about it. All resources held by the child process are

		released except for its process ID PID.
	X	EXIT_DEAD: The parent process has cleaned up the remains of the child process after it has exited; the child process has now been released completely. This state is rarely observed in utilities that list processes.

- ***Listing processes***

The current processes in the system can be listed using the **ps** command at the shell prompt.

The command provides detailed information about processes, which include:

- The UID user identification, which determines the privileges of the process
- The unique process ID PID
- The real-time usage of the CPU

- The allocated memory by the process in various locations of the system

- The location of the process STDOUT standard output, known as the controlling terminal

- The current state of the process

The option **aux** can be used with the ps command, which will display detailed information of all the processes.

It includes columns, which are useful to the user and also shows processes, which are without a controlling terminal.

If you use the long listing option **lax**, you will get some more technical details, but it may display faster skipping the lookup of the username.

If you run the ps command without any options, it will display processes, which have the same effective user ID EUID as that of the current user and associated with the same terminal where the ps command was invoked.

- The ps listing also shows zombies, which are either exiting or defunct

- ps command only shows one display.

    You can alternatively use the top command, which will keep repeating the display output in realtime

- Processes, which have round brackets are usually the ones run by kernel threads.

  They show up at the top of the listing

- The ps command can display a tree format so that you can understand the parent and child process relationships

- The default order in which the processes are listed is not sorted.

  They are listed in a manner where the first process started, and the rest followed.

  You may feel that the output is chronological, but there is no guarantee unless you explicitly use options like -O or --sort

  o **Controlling Jobs**

In this section, we will learn about the terms such as foreground, background, and the controlling terminal.

We will also learn about using job control, which will allow us to manage multiple command-line tasks.

  o *Jobs and Sessions*

Job control is a feature in the shell through which multiple commands can be managed by a single shell instance.

Every pipeline that you enter at the shell prompt is associated with a job.

All processes in this pipeline are a part of the job and are members of the same process group.

A minimal pipeline is when only a single command is entered on the shell prompt.

In such a case, that command ends up being the only member of the job.

At a given time, inputs given to the command line from a keyboard can be read by only one job.

That terminal is known as the controlling terminal, and the processes that are a part of that job are known as foreground processes.

If there is any other job associated with that controlling terminal of, which it is a member, it is known as the background process of that controlling terminal.

Inputs given from the keyboard to the terminal cannot be read by background processes, but they can still write to the terminal.

A background job can be in a stopped state or a running state.

If a background process tries to read from the terminal, the process gets automatically suspended.

Every terminal that is running is a session of its own and can have processes that are in the foreground and the background.

A job is a part of one session only, the session that belongs to its controlling terminal.

If you use the **ps** command, the listing will show the name of the device of the controlling terminal of a process in a column named **TTY**.

There are some processes started by the system, such as system daemons, which are not a part of the shell prompt.

Therefore, these processes are not part of a job, or they do not have a controlling terminal and will never come to the foreground.

Such processes, when listed using the ps command shows **?** mark in the TTY column.

- **Running Background Jobs**

You can add an ampersand **&** to the end of a command line, which will run the command in the background.

There will be a unique job number assigned to the job, and a process ID PID will be assigned to the child process, which is created in bash.

The shell prompt will show up again after the command is executed as the shell will not wait for the child process to complete since it is running in the background.

[student@desktop ~]$ sleep 10000 &

[1] 5683

[student@desktop ~]$

Note: When you are putting a pipeline in the background with an ampersand **&**, the process ID PID that will show up in the output will be that of the last command in the pipeline.

All other commands that precede will be a part of that job.

[student@desktop ~]$ example_command | sort |mail -s "sort output" &

[1] 5456

Jobs are tracked in the bash shell, per session, in the output table that is shown by using the **jobs** command.

[student@desktop ~]$ jobs

[1]+ Runningsleep10000 &

[student@desktop ~]$

You can use the **fg** command with a job ID(*%job number*) to bring a job from the background to the foreground.

[student@desktop ~]$ fg %1

sleep 10000

-

In the example seen above, we brought the sleep command, which was running in the background to the foreground on the controlling terminal.

The shell will go back to sleep until this child process completes.

This is why you will have to wait until the sleep command is over for the shell prompt to show up again.

You can send a process from the foreground to the background by pressing **Ctrl+z** on the keyboard, which will send a suspend request.

sleep 10000

^Z

[1]+Stoppedsleep10000

[student@desktop ~]$

The job will get suspended and will be placed in the background.

The information regarding jobs can be displayed using the **ps j** command.

The display will show a PGID, which is the PID of the process group leader and refers to the first job in the pipeline of the job.

The SID is the PID of the session leader, which with respect to a job, refers to the interactive shell running on the controlling terminal.

[student@desktop ~]$ ps j

PPID PID PGID SID TTY TPGID STAT UID TIME COMMAND

2434 2456 2456 2456 pts/0 5677 T 1000 0:00 sleep 10000

The status of the sleep command is T because it is in the suspended state.

You can start a suspended process again in the background and put it into a running state by using the **bg** command with the same job ID.

[student@desktop ~]$ bg %1

[1]+ sleep 10000 &

[student@desktop ~]$

If there are jobs that are suspended and you try to exit the shell, you will get a warning that will let you know that there are suspended jobs in the background.

If you confirm to leave, the suspended jobs are killed immediately.

- o **Killing Processes**

In this section, we will learn how to use the command to communicate with processes and kill them.

We will understand what is a daemon process and what its characteristics are.

We will also learn how to end processes and sessions owned by a user.

- ***Using signals to control processes***

A signal is an interrupt developed through software to be sent to a process.

Events are sent to a program with the help of signals.

These events that generate a signal can be external events, errors, or explicit requests such as commands sent using the keyboard.

Let us go through a few signals, which are useful for system admins in their routine day to day system management activities.

Signal number	Short name	Definition	Purpose
1	HUP	Hangup	This signal reports the termination of the controlling process in a terminal.

				Process reinitialization or configuration reload can be requested using this signal without any termination.
2		INT	Keyboard Interrupt	This signal leads to the termination of a program. The signal can either be blocked or handled. The signal is sent by using the **Ctrl+c** on the keyboard known as **INTR**
3		QUIT	Keyboard quit	The signal is similar to **SIGINT** with the difference that a process dump is generated at termination. The signal is sent by using the **Ctrl+** on the keyboard known as **QUIT**
9		KILL	Kill, unblockable	This signal leads to an abrupt termination of the program.

			It cannot be blocked, handled, or ignored and is always fatal.
15 default	TERM	Terminate	This signal leads to the termination of the program. Unlike **SIGKILL,** this signal can be clocked, ignored, or handled. This is requesting a program to terminate in a polite way, which results in proper clean-up.
18	CONT	Continue	This signal is sent to a process that is in a stopped state such that it resumes. The signal cannot be blocked, and the process is resumed even if the signal is handled.
19	STOP	Stop, Unblockable	This signal leads to suspension of the process and cannot be handled or blocked.

| 20 | TSTP | Keyboard stop | Unlike **SIGSTOP,** this signal can be blocked, handled, or ignored. The signal is sent by using the **Ctrl+z** on the keyboard known as **SUSP** |

Note: The number of signal numbers can change based on the hardware being used for the Linux operating system, but the signal names and their purposes are standardized.

Therefore, it is advisable that you use the signal names instead of the signal number on the command line.

The signal numbers are only for systems that are associated with the Intel x86 architecture.

There is a default action associated with every signal, which corresponds to one of the following.

Term - The program is asked to exit or terminate at once.

Core - The program is asked to terminate but is asked to also save a memory image or a core dump before terminating.

Stop - the program is suspended or asked to stop and will have to wait to resume again.

Expected event signals can be tackled by programs by implementing routines for handlers so that they can replace, ignore, or extend the default action of a signal.

Commands used to send signals through explicit requests

Processes that are running in the foreground can be signaled using the keyboard by users, wherein control signals are sent to the process using keys like Ctrl+z for suspending, Ctrl+c for kill, and Ctrl+\ for getting a core dump.

If you want to send signals to processes that are running in the background or are running in a different session altogether, you will need to use a command to send signals.

You can either use signal names(-HUP or -SIGHUP) to signal numbers(-1) to specify a signal.

Processes, which are owned by a user, can be killed by the users themselves, but processes owned by others will need root user privileges to be killed.

- The **kill** command can be sent to a process using the process ID PID.

However, irrespective of the name, the kill command can be used to send other signals to a process as well and not just for sending a signal to terminate the process.

```
[student@desktop ~]$ kill PID

[student@desktop ~]$ kill -signal PID
```

- The **killall** command can be used to send a signal to multiple processes, which may match given criteria such as processes owned by a particular user, command name, all system processes.

```
[student@desktop ~]$ killall command_pattern

[student@desktop ~]$ killall -signal command_pattern

[student@desktop ~]$ killall -signal -u username command_pattern
```

- Just like the **killall** command, there is another command called **pkill, which** can be used to signal multiple processes at the same time.

The selection criteria used by pkill is advanced in comparison to killall and contains the following combinations.

Command - Pattern that is matched using the command name

UID - Processes that belong to a particular user matched using UID

GID - Processes that belong to a particular group matched using GID

Parent - Child processes that belong to a particular parent process

Terminal - Processes that are running on a particular controlling terminal

[student@desktop ~]$ pkill command_pattern

[student@desktop ~]$ pkill -signal command_pattern

[root@desktop ~]# pkill -G GID command_pattern

[root@desktop ~]# pkill -P PPID command_pattern

[root@desktop ~]# pkill -t terminal_name -U UID command_pattern

- ***Administratively logging out users***

The **w** command lists down all the users that are logged into the system and the processes that are being run by these users.

You can determine the location of the users by analyzing the **FROM** and the **TTY** columns.

Every user is associated with a controlling terminal, which is indicated by **pts/N** while working on a graphical interface or

ttyN while working on a system console where **N** is the number of the controlling terminal.

Users who have connected remotely to the system will be displayed in the **FROM** column when you use the **-f** option.

[student@desktop ~]$ w -f

12:44:34 up 25 min, 1 users, load average: 0.06, 0.45, 0.55

USERTTYFROMLOGIN@IDLEJCPUPCPUWHAT

student pts/0:012:322.02s0.07s   0.07s   w -f

The session login time will let you know as to how long a user has been on the system.

The CPU resources that are utilized by current jobs, including the child processes and background jobs, are shown in the JCPU column. CPU utilization for foreground processes is shown in the PCPU column.

If a user is violating the security of the system, or over-allocating resources, they can be forced out of the system.

Therefore, if the system admin is requesting a user to close processes that are not required, close command shells that are unused, exit login sessions, they are supposed to follow the system admin.

In situations where a user is out of contact and has ongoing sessions, which are putting a load on the system by consuming resources, a system admin may need to administratively end their session.

Note: The signal to be used in this case is **SIGTERM,** but most system admins use **SIGKILL, which** can be fatal. The SIGKILL signal cannot be handled or ignored; it is fatal.

Processes are forced to terminate without completing clean-up routines.

Therefore, we recommend that you send the SIGTERM signal first before trying the SIGKILL signal when the process is not responding.

The signal can be sent individually or collectively to terminal or processes.

You can use the **pkill** command to terminate all processes for a particular user.

If you want to kill all the processes of a user and all their login shells, you will need to use the **SIGKILL** signal.

This is because the session leader process, which is the initial process in a session, can handle session termination requests and other signals coming from the keyboard.

[root@desktop ~]# pgrep -l -u alice

6787 bash

6789 sleep

6999 sleep

7000 sleep

[root@desktop ~]# pkill -SIGKILL -u alice

[root@desktop ~]# pgrep -l -u alice

[root@desktop ~]#

If you need certain processes by a user and only want to kill a few of their other processes, it is not necessary to kill all their processes.

Use the **w** command and figure out the controlling terminal for the session and then use the terminal ID to kill processes from a terminal, which is not required.

The session leader, which is the bash login shell, will survive the termination command unless you use the SIGKILL command, but this will terminate all other session processes.

[root@desktop ~]# pgrep -l -u alice

6787 bash

6789 sleep

6999 sleep

7000 sleep

[root@desktop ~]# w -h -u alice

alicetty318:545:070.45s0.34s-bash

[root@desktop ~]# pkill -t tty3

[root@desktop ~]# pgrep -l -u alice

6787 bash

[root@desktop ~]# pkill SIGKILL -t tty3

[root@desktop ~]# pgrep -l -u alice

The criteria of terminating processes selectively can also be applied by using arguments of relationships between parent and child processes.

The **pstree** command can be used in this case.

The pstree command shows a process tree for a user or for the system.

You can kill all its child processes by passing the parent process's parent ID PID.

The bash login shell of the parent process still remains since only the child processes are terminated.

[root@desktop ~]# pstree -u alice

bash(8341)sleep(8454)

sleep(8457)

sleep(8459)

[root@desktop ~]# pkill -P 8341

[root@desktop ~]# pstree -l -u alice

bash(8341)

[root@desktop ~]# pkill -SIGKILL -P 8341

[root@desktop ~]# pstree -l -u alice

bash(8341)

[root@desktop ~]#

- **Process Monitoring**

In this section, we will learn how to monitor processes in real-time and how to interpret load averages on the CPU of the system.

- *Load Average*

The Linux kernel is capable of calculating a **load average** metric, which is the **exponential moving average** of the **load number**, a cumulative count of the CPU that is kept in accordance with the system resources that are active in that given instance.

- Threads that are currently running or threads that are waiting for input or output are counted as the active requests in the CPU queue.

Meanwhile, the kernel keeps track of the activity of process resources and the changes in the state of the process.

- The calculation routine run by default in the system at an interval of every five seconds is known as load number.

  The load number will accumulate and average out all the active requests into one single number for every CPU.

- The mathematical formula used to smoothen the highs and lows of trending data, the increase in the one-word significance of the current activity, and decrease in the quality of aging data is known as the exponential moving average.

- The result of the routine load number calculation is known as the load average.

  It refers to the display of 3 figures, which show the load averages for 1, 5, and 15 minutes.

Let us try and understand how the load average calculation works in Linux systems.

The load average is a perception of the load received by the system over a period of time.

Along with CPU, the load average calculation also takes into consideration the disk and the network input and output.

- Linux systems do not just count processes.

    The threads of a process are also counted individually and account for as different tasks.

    The requests to CPU queues for running threads(nr_running) and threads that are waiting for I/O resources(nr_iowait) correspond to the process states of R Running and D Uninterruptible Sleeping.

    Tasks that may be sleeping are waiting for responses from disk, and networks are included in tasks waiting for Input/Output I/O.

- All the CPUs of the system are taken into consideration, and there the load number is known as the global counter for calculation.

    We cannot have counts that are accurate per CPU as tasks, which were initially sleeping, may be assigned to a different CPU when they resume.

    Therefore, we go for a count that has cumulative accuracy.

    The load average that is displayed represents all the CPUs.

- Linux will count each physical core of the CPU and microprocessor hyperthread as an execution unit, and therefore as an individual CPU.

  The request queues for each CPU is independent.

  You can check the /proc/cpuinfo file, which has all the information about the CPUs.

[root@desktop ~]# grep "model name" /proc/cpuinfo

model name: Intel(R) Core(TM) i5 CPUM 2600 @ 2.60GHz

model name: Intel(R) Core(TM) i7 CPUM 2600 @ 3.60GHz

model name: Intel(R) Core(TM) i7 CPUM 2600 @ 3.60GHz

model name: Intel(R) Core(TM) i7 CPUM 2600 @ 3.60GHz

[root@desktop ~]# grep "model name" /proc/cpuinfo |wc -l

- Previously known UNIX systems used to consider only CPU load or the length of the run queue to calculate the system load.

But soon it was realized that a system would have CPUs that may be idle, but the other resources like disk and network could be busy, and it was factored into the load average shown in modern Linux systems.

If the load average is high despite minimal CPU activity, you may want to have a look at the disk and the network.

Let us now learn how we can interpret the values shown for load averages.

This is an important part of being a system admin.

As we have already seen, you will see three values, which are the load values over a time period of 1, 5, and 15 minutes.

Having a quick look at these three values is enough to understand whether the load on the system is increasing or decreasing.

We can then calculate the approximate value per CPU load, which will let us know if the system is experiencing severe wait time.

- You can use the command-line utilities of **top, uptime, w,** and **gnome-system-monitor** to display values of average load.

- [root@desktop ~]# uptime

15:30:45up14 min,2 users,load average: 2.56, 4.56, 5.76

- You can now divide the load average values that you see by the number of logical CPUs that are present in the system.

If the result shows a value below 1, it implies that resource utilization and wait times are minimal.

If the value is above 1, it indicates that resources are saturated and that there is waiting time.

- If the CPU queue is idle, then the load number will be 0.

Threads that are waiting or ready will add a count of 1 to the queue.

If the total count on the queue is 1, resources of CPU, disk, and network are busy, but there is no waiting time for other requests.

With every additional request, the count increases by 1, but since many requests can be executed simultaneously, the resource utilization goes up, but there is no wait time for other requests.

- The load average increases by processes that may be in the sleeping state since they are waiting for input or output, but the disk and the network are busy.

Although this does not mean that the CPU is being utilized, it still means that there are processes and users waiting for system resources.

- The load average will stay below 1 until all the resources begin to get saturated as tasks are seldom found to be waiting in the queue.

It is only when requests start getting queued and are counted by the calculation routine that the load average starts spiking up.

Every additional request coming in will start experiencing wait time when the resource utilization touches 100 percent.

  o ***Process monitoring in Real-time***

Much like the **ps** command, the **top** command gives a dynamic view of the processes in the system, which shows a header summary and list of threads and processes.

The difference is that the output in the ps command is static in nature and just gives a one time output.

The output of the top command is dynamic and keeps refreshing the values in real-time.

The interval at which the values refresh can be customized.

You can also configure other things such as sorting, column reordering, highlighting, etc. and these user configurations can be saved and are persistent.

The default output columns are as follows.

- The process ID **PID**

- The process owner that is the user name **USER**

- All the memory that is used by a process **VIRT**, which includes memory used by shared libraries, resident set, and memory pages that may be mapped or swapped.

- The physical memory used by a process known as resident memory **RES, which** includes memory used by shared objects.

- The state of the process **S** displays as

D: Uninterruptible Sleeping

R: Running or Runnable

S: Sleeping

T: Traced or Stopped

Z: Zombie

- The total processing time since the process began is known as CPU time **TIME**. It can be toggled to show the cumulative time of all the previous child processes.

- The command name process **COMMAND**

Let us now go through some keystrokes that are helpful for system admins while using the top display.

Key	Purpose
? or h	Display the help section
l, t, m	Header lines of memory, load and threads are toggled
1	Toggle to show individual CPU or all CPUs
s	Change the refresh rate of the screen in seconds

| b | The default for the running process is a bold highlight.

These toggles reverse highlighting |
|---|---|
| B | Bold can be enabled in the header, display, and for running processes |
| H | Used to toggle threads to show individual threads or a summary of the processes |
| u, U | Used to filter for a username |
| M | Processes are sorted by memory usage in descending order |
| P | Processes are sorted by processor usage in descending order |
| k | Kills a process. When prompted, enter PID and signal |
| r | Renice a process. When prompted, enter PID and nice_value |
| w | Save or write the current display configuration when you launch top again |

| q | Quit |

Chapter 10: Manual Pages

Most people may not be able to know the wealth of power and opportunity that comes with the use of the Linux command line.

Maybe because they are afraid to use this system.

If you have a memory more or less like mine, the truth is that you experience a huge challenge recalling details.

However, lucky enough, we have a system that is easy to use and gets so much information about things we can do on the command line.

This is the main thing we are going to learn in this section.

First, let us begin by learning how to use manual pages.

So what are they exactly?

Manual pages refer to a set of pages that gives a detailed explanation of each and every command that is available on the system.

They also give details about what the command does, specific information on how to run them as well as the command arguments that they accept.

To be honest, some of them are rather challenging to understand and wrap our heads around.

However, the good thing is that they are consistent in their structure.

This means that once you have wrapped your head around, they are not as bad as they might seem/sound.

Searching

I know you might be wondering whether there is a possibility of performing a search on the manual pages.

Well, this is something that is very important, especially when you are not quite certain of the commands to use but are aware of the task you would like to achieve.

In order for this approach to be effective, you might need a number of tries.

This is because it is quite commanded to find that a particular word is represented many times in the manual pages.

This means that if you would wish to search within a manual page, it is quite possible.

In order to do this while on a certain manual page to search, the first thing that you have to do is to press the forward-slash on your keyboard and then type the term you would like to search.

Then press enter.

In a situation where the term is represented several times, you can navigate to the next one by simply tabbing the 'n' button to represent next.

For you to be proficient in Linux, the first thing that you have to understand is what command-line options are used in the modification of the behavior of other commands in order to successfully perform the tasks that we intend to.

Most of these have both a long and shorthand.

For instance, you can use the command line option –a or --all.

But, they both perform the same functions.

The long hand is just a format that is more readable to humans.

The main advantage of using the long hand option is that it makes it much easier for you to recall what the command does.

However, learned, the advantage of using the shorthand is the fact that you can put together multiple commands in an easy manner.

Consider the following example:

    meenu@bash:pwd

    /home/Linusss

    meenu@bash:ls -a

    meenu@bash:ls --all

```
meenu@bash:ls -alh
```

When you look up at the manual page for the ls command, you will be able to know what other commands do.

You will realize that the long hand command options begin with two dashes while the shorthand command option starts with a single dash.

Whenever we use a single dash, we invoke a number of options by simply placing all the letters that represent that option together to come after the dash.

In order to summarize what we have learned in this section, we will recap the commands we have learned and what roles they play.

man <command> is used to look up the manual page of commands.

For example, man ls is used to look up the manual page for the list command.

man –k <search term> is used to perform a keyword search for the manual pages that have the search term.

/<term> is used to perform a search for a term within a manual page

n is used to navigate to the next item in the manual page after performing a search.

The most important thing that you have to know is that for you to be a guru in Linux, you have to make the manual pages your friends.

This is the easiest way to find the commands and the role they play instead of cracking your mind to recall stuff when the computer can simply do it for you!

Practice activities

Now that we have learned a little bit more, let us give the following a try:

Skim through the manual pages for the ls command.

Try out some of the command-line options that are presented there and take note of what they do.

Ensure that while at it, you play with a few combinations using both the relative and the absolute path.

Now, I would like you to perform a number of searches through the manual pages.

Based on the chosen terms, you may have a long list as you want.

Take a look at a number of pages and get a feel of what they look or feel like.

Chapter 11: Manipulating Files and Directories

Now that you've got your hands a little dirty, you must be eager to get on to some more coding and really get down to playing about in the system.

You will, I promise, but first, there is some more theory that you really need to learn so that, when you do get into the system, you truly understand why it does what it does and how to do more with the commands you have learned.

So, let's take a deeper look at the core concepts you need to learn.

Access Rights

Rights or permissions allow certain users or groups of users to restrict access to specific files or directories.

There are three types of access rights:

- Read (r) for reading access to the file (allows the printing, displaying, and copying of a file and allows traversing the directory or displaying files in a directory)

- Write (w) for write access to the file (allows the modification of a file, and allows the deletion of a file or the saving of a file in a directory)

- Execute (x) for the possibility of executing the file (allows the execution of a program, a executable, and enables to access the management information of the files of the directory, like the inode, the table of the rights).

For each file, access rights are set for three categories of users:

- user (u): the owner of the filegroup
- filegroup (g): the group that owns the file
- all (a): all users

To view the rights of all files in the current directory:

Ls –la, the access rights can also be expressed in their octal form, that is to say, using a number from 0 to 7 (there are eight possibilities, which can be fixed with only 3 bits).

Each of the rights (r, w, and x) corresponds to an octal value (4, 2, and 1), the octal values are accumulated for each type of user (u, g, and o).

For each type of user (u, g, o), the value in octal can take the benefits 0, 1, 2, 3, 4, 5, 6, and 7.

For example, the combination of all rights cumulated for three types of users (rwx rwx rwx) is equivalent to the octal value 777.

- 0 means no rights
- 1 is the executable right (--x)
- 2 is the write right (-w-)
- 3 corresponds to the cumulative execution and writing rights (-wx)
- 4 corresponds to the right of reading (r--)
- 5 is the collective read and execute rights (rx)
- 6 corresponds to the aggregate rights of reading and writing (rw-)
- 7 is the collective read, write and execute rights (rwx)

For example:

666 gives the right to all read and write

764 gives all rights to all

700 gives all rights to the file owner

The octal number can be four digits when the superuser sets the exclusive rights ("s" and "t").

File Naming Rules Old Unixes

We're limited to 14 characters, but nowadays, long file names are handled from 1 to 255 characters.

The slash (/) is forbidden because it is the directory delimiter in the tree, and represents the root, i.e the top of the tree.

Files whose names began with a period are hidden or hidden files.

They do not appear by default with the "ls" command without the "- a" option, and most commands do not take them into account less than mention it explicitly.

The double dot (..) identifies the parent directory, and the dot (.) identifies the current directory or working directory.

These two files exist in all directories.

It is, therefore, not possible to name a file with a single point or with two points since the pointers already exist (it is not possible to have two files with the same name in the same directory, and it is not possible that you cannot delete the pointer to the current directory or the parent directory).

Everything in Linux is a file.

This is a very important concept to grasp—everything in Linux, no matter where it's or what it does, is a file.

Text files are, obviously, files. Directories are files.

Your computer keyboard is a read-only file, the monitor on your computer—even this is a file, albeit a write-to file.

Everything. To start with, this won't have any real effect on what you do, but you must always keep it in mind as it will help you to grasp how Linux works with directory and file management.

Linux is known as an "extensionless system."

This one is a little bit harder to grasp, but as you work through this book and learn more, you'll find that it makes sense.

File extensions are usually made up of a series of 2, 3, or 4 characters after a dot.

You've already seen these with Word (.doc, .docx), .pdf, and so on.

This extension is what tells you the type of file you are working with.

These are some of the more common ones that you'll come across:

- *File.exe*: a program or a file that's executable
- *File.txt*: a file in plain text
- **File.png, file.jpg, file.gif:** *all image files*

In many systems, like Windows, this file extension is very important because the system will use it to work out what kind of file it's working with. In Linux, it's different.

The Linux system will ignore that extension and, instead, it will investigate the file itself to see what it's to do.

So, for example, you could have a file that's named monkey.gif, a picture of a monkey.

You could give the file a new name, such as monkey.txt or even just monkey, and Linux will see it as the image file it really is.

Because of this, you might sometimes find it difficult to determine what type a file is, but there is a really easy way to find out in Linux by using one simple command: file.

file [path]

Now, you are probably asking yourself why the command line argument is a path and not a file.

If you think back, remember that every directory or file that we specify on the command line is a path.

And, because a directory is also a file, it's correct to say that the path is nothing more than a journey to a system location, and the location is the file.

Linux is case sensitive.

This is one of the most important concepts and is the one that tends to cause the most problems for those new to the Linux program.

You already know that systems like Windows are case insensitive in terms of file referencing, but Linux is different.

You can have multiple directories or files with identical names but different cases.

For example:

ls Documents

FILE2.txt File2.txt file2.TXT

...

file Documents/file2.txt

Documents/file2.txt: ERROR: cannot open 'file2.txt' (No such file or directory)

Each one of these is seen as an individual file by Linux.

Case sensitivity also comes into command-line options.

For example, when you use the command ls, there are two distinct options: ls and lS, and both do something different.

One of the more common errors is to enter an option in lowercase when it should be uppercase, and then wonder why your program doesn't do what it should.

Spaces in file or directory names

While it's perfectly okay to have spaces in your directory or file names, you must exercise some small measure of caution.

When we want to separate several items on the command line, we use a space between each one.

The spaces are what tell us what the program name is and how to identify the different arguments on the command line.

For example, if we wanted to go into a directory that we called Summer Holiday, this next example would not work:

ls Documents

FILE2.txt File2.txt file2.TXT Summer Holiday

…

cd Summer Holiday

bash: cd: Holiday: No such file or directory

Why not?

Well, Summer Holiday is seen by Linux as 2 separate command line arguments, so the command, cd, will go into the first one only.

The only way to stop this from happening is to tell the terminal that Summer Holiday is just one argument, and there are two ways to do this, both of which are perfectly valid.

Quotes

The first way involves surrounding the whole item with quote marks.

You can use singles or doubles (although there is a small difference between the two), but do make sure that you use the same to open as you do to close the quote marks.

For example, don't open with a single quote and then close with a double.

Anything that goes inside those quotes is then seen as one item, for example:

cd 'Summer Holiday'

pwd

/home/cleopatra/Documents/Summer Holiday

Escape characters

The other way is using an escape character, the backslash (\).

The escape character will nullify or escape the special meaning attached to the following character, for example:

cd Holiday\ Photos

pwd

/home/cleopatra/Documents/Summer Holiday

As you can see from this example, the space that separates Summer and Holiday would usually have a special meaning: to separate each work as a separate command-line argument.

By using the escape character, we removed that meaning, and the two words are one argument.

Earlier, we talked about something called TAB completion.

If you were to use this before you get to a space in the name of a directory, the terminal escapes the spaces automatically.

Hidden directories and files

Linux has a very nice way of specifying whether a directory or a file is hidden or not.

If the name starts with a. (a followed by a full stop), it's a hidden directory or file.

There are no requirements for special commands or special actions to hide them.

There are several reasons why you may want to hide a directory or a file, and one of those is if they relate to the configuration for a specific user.

These can be hidden so they don't interfere with everyday tasks that the user may be doing.

So, if you want to hide a file or a directory, simply create it or rename it with the name beginning with a.

In the same way, if you wanted to unhide a directory or file, you would simply rename it, removing the a. from the start of the name.

The command that you learned to list directories and files will NOT show those that are hidden.

Instead, you can modify the command to add in -a as a command-line option, allowing those hidden files and directories to be shown.

ls Documents

FILE2.txt File2.txt file2.TXT

...

ls -a Documents

. .. FILE2.txt File2.txt file2.TXT .hidden .file.txt

...

In this example, you can see that, when the directories and files were listed, the first two were . and then .. and if you need to brush up on those head back to the section on paths.

Summary

Here's a quick summary of what you learned in this section:

- "File" is used to get information about the type of a directory or file.

- "ls –a" lists all files in a directory, including those that are hidden.

- Everything is a file in Linux, including directories.

- File extensions are not important because Linux will investigate the file to see what it is.

- Linux is a case-sensitive language, so watch out for capitalization.

Practical work

Now we need to put it all into practice, so try these:

- Run the command file with several different entries and ensure that you use a combination of absolute and relative paths.

- Next, give a command that will show everything that's in your home directory, including any directories or files that are hidden.

More on running commands

Much of understanding Linux is down to knowing the right command-line options to use to change how your commands work, based on what you are doing with them.

Many of these will have a long and shorthand version; for example, we saw earlier that, when we want to list everything in a directory, including hidden entries, we use -a or --all.

The longhand version is just a version that's easily read by the human eye.

You can use either of these because they both have the same outcome.

The advantage to longhand is that, when you read back over your code, you'll find it easier to understand what the commands do while using shorthand allows you to string several commands together easily.

pwd

/home/cleopatra

ls -a

ls --all

ls -alh

So, you can see that the longhand options each start with a pair of dashes (--), while the shorthand options all start with a single dash (-).

When you use the single dash, you can invoke several command options by adding all the letters that represent those options after a single dash.

To see what the last option is doing, look up the main ls page.

Man pages

These are the commands for looking up main manual pages:

- *man <command>*: looks up the manual page for a command
- *man -k <search term>*: use a keyword to search for all pages that have the keyword in them
- */<term>*: used in a manual page to search for the word "term"
- *n:* after the search is done on a page, choose the next item found
- Remember: man pages are useful, so use them as often as you need to.

    You don't need to try and remember everything when you have these at your disposal.

Practical work

Try the following to get some practice:

Look through the manual page for the ls command.

Play around with some of the options you see there and try some of them as combinations.

Don't forget to use a variety of relative and absolute paths with the ls command.

Now have a go at some searches in the man pages.

Depending on what you search for, you could end up with a few large lists.

Look at some of the pages to get an idea of what they are.

Removing a directory

As you have seen, it's easy to create a new directory, and it's just as easy to remove or delete a directory too.

There is one thing you should be aware of, though—the Linux command line doesn't contain any UNDO options.

This means being very careful about what you are doing because once you delete a directory, it's gone forever.

To remove a directory, we use a simple command of rmdir, which is shorthand for remove directory.

rmdir [options] <Directory>

There are two more things that you need to note here.

First, in a similar way to how mkdir (make directory) supports the options -v and -p, rmdir also supports those options.

Second, before you can remove a directory, it must be empty.

However, there is a way around this, and we will look at that later.

rmdir linuxpractice/foo/bar

ls linuxpractice/foo

Creating blank files

There are quite a few commands for data manipulation in files that, if you refer to a file that doesn't exist, will create that file for you.

We can use this to create a blank file by using the touch command.

touch [options] <filename>

pwd

/home/cleopatra/linuxpractice

ls

foo

touch showcase1

ls

showcase1 foo

We can use the touch command to alter the times for accessing the file and its modification.

This isn't something you would need to do unless you are testing your given system with a reliance on these access rules and modification times.

Basically, what happens here—and this is something you make good use of—is that, when you touch a file that doesn't exist, it will be created for you.

There are a lot of things that are not directly done in Linux but, if you learn how certain commands behave and learn how to be creative with them, you can achieve what you want.

Right now, all we have is a blank file, but soon, we will look at how we can put data into a file and how to extract data as well.

Copy any given file/directory

You might create a copy of a directory or file—perhaps you want to make a change to something, so you would make a copy of the original.

That way, if anything goes wrong, you can easily go back to what it was.

To do this, we use the command cp, which means copy.

cp [options] <source> <destination>

This command has fewer options to it, and we're going to talk about one of them in a minute.

First though, check out the cp man page to see what other options are available.

ls

showcase1 foo

cp showcase1 sammy

ls

sammy showcase1 foo

Did you spot that the source and the destination are both paths?

What this means is that we can use absolute and relative paths to refer to them.

Have a look at these few examples:

cp /home/cleopatra/linuxpractice/showcase2 showcase3

cp showcase2 ../../backups

cp showcase2 ../../backups/showcase4

cp /home/cleopatra/linuxpractice/showcase2 /otherdir/foo/showcase5

So, when cp is used, the destination may be a path that goes to a directory or to a file.

If it goes to a file, as in the first, third, and fourth example lines above, a copy of the source will be created, and it will have the filename that was specified in the destination path.

If we were going to a directory, then the file would be copied to the directory and will be named the same as the source.

By default, cp can only copy a file so, if you wanted to copy a directory, you would need to use the option -r, which means recursive.

Recursive means looking into a directory, at the files and the directories contained in it.

To see the subdirectories, you do the same, but from within each directory.

ls

sammy showcase1 foo

cp foo foo2

cp: omitting directory 'foo'

cp -r foo foo2

ls

sammy showcase1 foo foo2

In this example, we're copying all the files and the directories from the foo directory to foo2.

Moving a file or directory

Moving a file is done quite simply with the mv command, which means move.

It works in much the same way as cp, except that we can use it without -r for moving directories.

mv [options] <source> <destination>

ls

sammy showcase1 foo foo2

mkdir backups

mv foo2 backups/foo3

mv sammy backups/

ls

backups showcase1 foo

Let's look at that in more detail:

Line 3: a new directory has been created with the name backups.

Line 4: the directory called foo2 was moved into the directory called backups and was renamed as foo3.

Line 7: the file called sammy was moved into the backups directory. It retained the same name because we didn't give a destination name.

Note that, once again, we used paths for source and destination, and these are absolute or relative paths.

Renaming your files and/or directories

The behavior of mv can also be used creatively to give us a different outcome.

Normally, we use mv to move files or directories into a newly-created directory.

Part of that move includes renaming that file or directory.

If we were to specify that the destination and the source are similar but named differently, that would be a creative use of mv for renaming directories or files.

ls

backups showcase1 foo

mv foo foo3

ls

backups showcase1 foo3

cd ..

mkdir linuxpractice/testdir

mv linuxpractice/testdir /home/cleopatra/linuxpractice/frieda

ls linuxpractice

backups showcase1 foo3 frieda

Let's delve into this one:

Line 3: the file called foo was given a new name of foo3. Both paths are relative.

Line 6: the parent directory was moved.

We did this so that in the next line, we could show how to run commands on a file or a directory from outside the directory they are contained in.

Line 8: the directory called testdir was renamed to frieda.

We used a relative path to the source and an absolute path to the destination.

Removing files

Like we saw with rmdir, when you remove a file, you cannot undo it, so take care with what you are doing.

The command for removing or deleting files is rm, which means remove.

rm [options] <file>

ls

backups showcase1 foo3 frieda

rm showcase1

ls

backups foo3 frieda

Removing directories that aren't empty

The command rm can also be altered by several different options.

Again, check out the rm man page to see what can be done, but one of the most useful options is -r.

Like cp, it means recursive, and we use it with rm to remove specified directories and everything that's contained inside them.

ls

backups foo3 frieda

rmdir backups

rmdir: did not manage to get rid of the 'backups': Directory not empty

rm backups

rm: cannot get rid of 'backups': Is a directory

rm -r backups

ls

foo3 frieda

Another option you can use with r is I meaning interactive.

This will check with you before any file or directory is removed and provide you with an option to change your mind and cancel out the command.

One last note

I have already said this a few times, and I will keep on saying it: when we refer, on the command-line, to files or directories, they are paths.

They may be absolute paths or relative paths, and this is going to be the case pretty much all the time.

I won't remind you of this again, and the examples I use will not show this, so please remember it.

Don't forget to practice with relative and absolute paths in your commands that we use, as each will provide different outputs.

Summary

This is some of what you learned in this section:

- *Mkdir*: stands for Make Directory and allows us to create new directories
- *Rmdir*: stands for Remove Directory and allows us to delete directories
- *Touch*: allows us to create blank files
- *Cp*: stands for Copy and allows us to copy directors or files
- *Mv*: stands for Move and allows us to move or rename files or directories
- *Rm*: stands for Remove and allows us to delete files

- There is no option to undo anything you do, so delete and move files and directories with care.

- Command-line options: there are plenty of them, so use the man pages of each command to familiarize yourself with what there is and what you can do

Practical work

You now have several different commands that will let you interact with your system, so let's practice with them.

Try the following:

- Create a brand new directory within the home directory (this will allow you to experiment).

- Inside the directory, create some files and some directories and create more files & any directories inside of each of those.

- Now give new names to some of them.

- Go to the home directory, copy one file from a subdirectory into the first directory that you created.

- Move the file to another directory.

- Take more files and rename them.

- Move one file and ensure it is renamed at the same time.

- Lastly, check directories that are already in the home directory.

  Most likely, you have Downloads, Documents, Images, and Music.

  Have a think about other directories that can help you to keep things organized and start to set them up.

Chapter 12: Advanced Working with Files

Here is the output from an ls command using the -l option.

The -l flag tells ls to display output in a long format.

If you need to see what files or directories exist, use ls. However, if you need detailed information, use ls -l.

$ ls -l

-rw-rw-r-- 1 December users 10400 Oct 23 08:52 sales.data

On the far left of the ls output is a series of characters that represent the file permissions.

The number that follows the permissions represents the number of links to the file.

The next bit of information is the owner of the file, followed by the group name.

Next, the file size is displayed, followed by the date and time when the file was last modified.

Finally, the name of the file or directory is displayed.

Here is the information displayed by the ls -l command in table form.

Item	Value
Permissions	-rw-rw-r--
Number of links	1
Owner name	bob
Group name	users
Bytes contained in file	10400
Last modification time	Oct 23 08:52
File name	sales.data

Listing All Files, Including Hidden Files

Files or directories that begin with a period (.) are considered hidden and are not displayed by default.

To show these hidden files and directories, use the -a option.

$ ls -a

..

.profile

.bash_history

lecture.mp3

PerfReviews

sales.data

tpsreports

Up until this point, when you have used options, you have preceded each option with a hyphen (-).

Examples are -l and -a.

Options that do not take arguments can be combined.

Only one hyphen is required followed by the options.

If you want to show a long ls listing with hidden files you could run ls -l -a or ls -la.

You can even change the order of the flags, so ls -al works too.

They are all equivalent.

$ ls -l

total 2525

-rw-r--r-- 1 December sales   25628 Oct 23 08:54 lecture.mp3

drwxr-xr-x 3 December users   512 Oct 24 09:20 PerfReviews

-rw-r--r-- 1 December users   10400 Oct 23 08:52 sales.data

drwxr-xr-x 2 December users   512 Oct 24 14:49 tpsreports

$ ls -l -a

total 2532

drwxr-xr-x 4 December sales   512 Oct 24 14:56 .

drwxr-xr-x 14 root root   512   Oct 23 08:43 ..

-rw-r--r-- 1 December users   28   Oct 24 14:22 .profile

-rw------- 1 December users 3314   Oct 24 14:56 .bash_history

-rw-r--r-- 1 December sales 25628 Oct 23 08:54 lecture.mp3

drwxr-xr-x 3 December users   512   Oct 24 09:20 PerfReviews

-rw-r--r-- 1 December users 10400 Oct 23 08:52 sales.data

drwxr-xr-x 2 December users   512   Oct 24 14:49 tpsreports

$ ls -la

total 2532

drwxr-xr-x 4 December sales   512   Oct 24 14:56 .

drwxr-xr-x 14 root root   512   Oct 23 08:43 ..

-rw-r--r-- 1 December users   28   Oct 24 14:22 .profile

-rw------- 1 December users 3314   Oct 24 14:56 .bash_history

-rw-r--r-- 1 December sales 25628 Oct 23 08:54 lecture.mp3

drwxr-xr-x 3 December users   512   Oct 24 09:20 PerfReviews

-rw-r--r-- 1 December users 10400 Oct 23 08:52 sales.data

drwxr-xr-x 2 December users   512   Oct 24 14:49 tpsreports

$ ls -al

total 2532

```
drwxr-xr-x  4 December sales  512   Oct 24 14:56 .
drwxr-xr-x 14 root     root   512   Oct 23 08:43 ..
-rw-r--r--  1 December users   28   Oct 24 14:22 .profile
-rw-------  1 December users 3314   Oct 24 14:56 .bash_history
-rw-r--r--  1 December sales 25628  Oct 23 08:54 lecture.mp3
drwxr-xr-x  3 December users  512   Oct 24 09:20 PerfReviews
-rw-r--r--  1 December users 10400  Oct 23 08:52 sales.data
drwxr-xr-x  2 December users  512   Oct 24 14:49 tpsreports
```

Listing Files by Type

When you use the -F option for ls a character is appended to the file name that reveals what type it is.

```
$ ls
dir1 link program regFile
$ ls -F
dir1/ link@ program* regFile
$ ls -lF
total 8
drwxr-xr-x 2 December users 117 Oct 24 15:31 dir1/
lrwxrwxrwx 1 December users   7 Oct 24 15:32 link@ -> regFile
```

-rwxr-xr-x 1 December users 10 Oct 24 15:31 program*

-rw-r--r-- 1 December users 750 Oct 24 15:32 regFile

Symbol	Meaning
/	Directory.
@	Link. The file that follows the -> symbol is the target of the link.
*	Executable program.

A link is sometimes called a symlink, short for a symbolic link.

A link points to the location of the actual file or directory.

You can operate on the link as if it were the actual file or directory.

Symbolic links can be used to create shortcuts to long directory names.

Another common use is to have a symlink point to the latest version of installed software, as in this example.

bob@linuxsvr:~$ cd /opt/apache

bob@linuxsvr:/opt/apache ~$ ls -F

2.3/ 2.4/ current@

bob@linuxsvr:/opt/apache$ ls -l

drwxr-xr-x 2 root root 4096 Sep 14 12:21 2.3

```
drwxr-xr-x 2 root root 4096 Nov 27 15:43 2.4
lrwxrwxrwx 1 root root    5 Nov 27 15:43 current -> 2.4
```

Listing Files by Time and in Reverse Order

If you would like to sort the ls listing by time, use the -t option.

```
$ ls -t
tpsreports
PerfReviews
lecture.mp3
sales.data
$ ls -lt
total 2532
drwxr-xr-x 2 December users     512  Oct 24 14:49 tpsreports
drwxr-xr-x 3 December users     512  Oct 24 09:20 PerfReviews
-rw-r--r-- 1 December sales  2562856 Oct 23 08:54 lecture.mp3
-rw-r--r-- 1 December users   10400  Oct 23 08:52 sales.data
```

When you have a directory that contains many files, it can be convenient to sort them by time, but in reverse order.

This will put the latest modified files at the end of the ls output.

The old files will scroll off the top of your display, but the most recent files will be right above your prompt.

$ ls -latr

total 2532

drwxr-xr-x 14 root root 512   Oct 23 08:43 ..

-rw-r--r-- 1 December users 10400 Oct 23 08:52 sales.data

-rw-r--r-- 1 December sales 256285 Oct 23 08:54 lecture.mp3

drwxr-xr-x 3 December users 512   Oct 24 09:20 PerfReviews

-rw-r--r-- 1 December users 28   Oct 24 14:22 .profile

drwxr-xr-x 2 December users 512   Oct 24 14:49 tpsreports

drwxr-xr-x 4 December sales 512   Oct 24 14:56 .

-rw------- 1 December users 3340 Oct 24 15:04 .bash_history

Listing Files Recursively

Using the -R option with ls causes files and directories to be displayed recursively.

$ ls -R

.:

PerfReviews lecture.mp3 sales.data tpsreports

./PerfReviews:

Fred John old

./PerfReviews/old:

Jane.doc

$

You can also use the tree command for a more visually appealing output.

If you only want to see the directory structure, use tree -d.

tree - List contents of directories in a tree-like format.

tree -d - List directories only.

tree -C - Colorize output.

$ tree

```
.
├── PerfReviews
│   ├── Fred
│   ├── John
│   └── old
│       └── Jane.doc
├── sales.data
├── sales-lecture.mp3
```

```
└── tpsreports
```

2 directories, 6 files

```
$ tree -d
.
└── PerfReviews
    └── old
```

2 directories

$

List Directories, Not Contents

Normally when you run ls against a directory, the contents of that directory are displayed.

If you want to ensure you only get the directory name, use the -d option.

```
$ ls -l PerfReviews
total 3
-rw-r--r-- 1 December users  36 Oct 23 08:49 Fred
-rw-r--r-- 1 December users  36 Oct 24 09:21 John
drwxr-xr-x 2 December users 512 Oct 23 12:40 old
$ ls -ld PerfReviews
```

```
drwxr-xr-x 3 December users 512 Oct 24 09:20 PerfReviews
```

```
$ ls -d PerfReviews
```

PerfReviews

Commonly Used ls Options

Here is a recap of the ls options you have learned.

Option	Description
-a	All files, including hidden files
--color	List files with colorized output
-d	List directory names and not their contents
-l	Long format
-r	Reverse order
-R	List files recursively
-t	Sort by time, most recently modified first

Working with Spaces in Names

If you want to make your life easier when working from the command line, do not use spaces in file and directory names.

Hyphens (-) or underscores (_) can be good substitutes for spaces.

CamelCase, the practice of capitalizing each word, is another good option.

For example, instead of naming your latest literary attempt, "the next great American novel.txt," you could use "the-next-great-american-novel.txt," "the_next_great_american_novel.txt," or even "TheNextGreatAmericanNovel.txt."

Sooner or later, you will encounter a file or directory that contains a space in the name.

There are two ways to deal with this.

The first is to use quotation marks.

Even though the file name is a file, operate on it using "a file."

The second option is to escape the space.

Escaping is like using quotes, but for single characters.

The escape symbol is \, also known as a backslash.

To escape a space, precede the space with the backslash (\) character.

$ ls -l

-rw-r--r-- 1 December users 18 Oct 2 05:03 a file

$ ls -l a file

ls: a: No such file or directory

ls: file: No such file or directory

$ ls -l "a file"

-rw-r--r-- 1 December users 18 Oct 2 05:03 a file

$ ls -l a\ file

-rw-r--r-- 1 December users 18 Oct 2 05:03 a file

$ ls -lb a*

-rw-r--r-- 1 December users 18 Oct 2 05:03 a\ file

$

The -b option to ls causes it to print escape codes.

Note that quoting and escaping not only applies to spaces, but with other special characters as well, including | & ' ; ( ) < > space tab.

Chapte 13: Text Editors

Linux distributions are comprised of a number of applications, referred to as text editors.

They can be used to develop text files or edit system configuration files.

These editors are similar to word processing programs.

However, normally it has fewer features, works only with text files, and may or may not support checking of spelling and formatting.

These text editors have some features and are simple to use.

They are normally found on all Linux distributions.

The number of editors installed over your system is based on which software packages you have installed on the system.

<u>Reasons Why You Should Use Text Editors</u>

Linux is a highly file-centric operating system, which means that everything is a file.

All fundamental configurations are done through carefully designed text files in the correct place with the correct content.

You can find many graphical tools for configuring Linux box.

However, the majority of these just twist files for you.

The text files have a specific syntax that you need to follow.

A simple character that is omitted can expose your system to risk.

Using a word processor for this is not a good idea.

This can actually corrupt your files with additional formatting information.

File configuration does not require italic or bold fonts; it just requires correct information.

The same thing applies to the source code.

Compilers are strict regarding syntax.

Few of them also consider where the particular command is.

Word processors will mess up the text position in the lines of code.

It is essential for you to have a clear understanding of what is in the source code or configuration file, to know whether the system will understand exactly what you are writing.

If you are considering coding, then you will want to use an Integrated Development Environment.

With this, it can help you write code more efficiently because it can predict what you would like to type, suggest changes, or also show your mistakes.

This can color specific keywords and automatically place things in the correct place.

The coloring and highlighting are done within the display.

These kinds of changes are done to the text files that are meant to be the plain text.

It is one of the best features that you cannot get with word processing programs, and this is required for text editing.

Conventionally, most Linux distributions just stick to install the editors like Vim and Emacs, as they are cursor-based and easy to use.

Vim is the advanced version of Vi text editor that was employed on the Unix system.

These editors are user-friendly, and they let the user work with ease on the cursor-based operations allowing to give a full-screen format.

These kinds of editors do not require any X Window system support and can be initiated from the shell command line.

However, in this mode, the working is not that easy because of the fact that there are no menus, mouse-click options, and scroll bars.

Although, KDE and GNOME support the text editors with all the vital features.

Using the text editors with the desktop environments is just like working on Windows and Macintosh systems.

They provide the user with full mouse support, elaborative and exciting menus, and scroll bars.

You may find these editors much easier to use as compared to Vi and Emacs.

The editors can run on either desktop environments, whether it is KDE or GNOME.

You must have pre-installed environments to use the editors.

Linux Text Editors

Linux has many text editors available when it comes to simple text, structured text, and programming languages.

Here are some of the most popular listed, and all of these are available for a wide range of operating systems.

Linux Text Editors For Plain Text

Linux text editors for plain text are segregated into two categories that are graphical editors.

The two categories are GUI and console text editors.

The benefit of the GUI editor is that it is an intuitive, user-friendly interface.

On the other hand, the advantage of the console text editor is the suitability for long-distance network connection, which may or may not offers appropriate bandwidth or reliability.

Console Based Text Editors

Emacs

This text editor supports the concept that more is better.

It is something that tries to support all features as far as possible.

In case you want power, then try Emacs.

Through this, you can actually get unrestricted open files and sub-windows, shell access, and immoral way with scripts you can call out the keywords, are defining features of Emacs.

There are many variations of Emacs available that are suitable for major programming languages used for text highlighting of programming keywords as it is done for coding.

When you have an Emacs session open, you can write, code, email, or also play arcade games.

Along with that, Emacs has its own onboard assistance system with excessive capabilities that are comprised of the user-defined development of new commands that you will never require leaving.

Some of the good things about this are that it is powerful, customizable, and extensible.

This allows you to express your own creativity.

Jed

Jed is one of the text editors that support menus and other GUI features in the console-based terminal.

This text editor mainly focuses on software development.

One of the best features is that it is rich in Unicode mode.

It is also extremely lightweight, which means that it will not exert pressure on the system resource, making it ideal for older systems.

Pico

The Pico text editor was developed to assist users in speeding their email along with the pine email system.

This text editor has lots of commands available, which is displayed at the bottom of the text editing area to help.

It is very easy to use, and it offers many basic features like paragraph justification, spelling checker, and copy/paste.

The interface is pretty much similar to that of Notepad in Windows.

Nano

The Nano text editor is done over small and amazing design goals for making an open-source version of Pico.

There are some additional features, such as search, replace, and smooth scrolling.

This editor also lets you use a mouse and other printer devices for positioning the cursor or activate commands over the shortcuts bar at the bottom of the screen.

It is keyboard-oriented, and you can perform many functions using the Control (Ctrl) keys.

Vim

Vim is one of the console-based plain text editors that supports syntax highlighting and has many plug-ins for specialized features and configurations.

It is one of the standard Linux editors.

This has been a part of Linux from the beginning.

It is possible to duct in and duct out in just a few seconds, which rapidly changes the text files.

More recent Vim extensions provide additional functionality comprising of new editing commands and mouse support and graphical versions.

You can find a tutorial for beginners, which is built-in and can be accessed through 'vimtutor' command.

Vim user manual is also available, which enlists the features.

It can be accessed either within Vim or online.

Chapter 14 : Edit your Files using Vim

One of the most interesting things about Linux is that it is designed and developed in a way where all information is stored in text-based files.

There are two types of text files, which are used in Linux.

Flat files in, which text is stored in rows containing similar information, which you will find in the /etc directory, and Extensible Markup Language (XML) file, which have text stored using tags, which you will find in the /etc and /usr directories.

The biggest advantage of text files is that they can be transferred from one system or platform to another without having the need to convert them, and they can also be viewed and edited using simple text editors.

Vim is the most popular text editor across all Linux flavors and is an improved version of the previously popular vi editor.

Vim can be configured as per the needs of a user and includes features like color formatting, split-screen editing, and highlighting text for editing.

Vim works in 4 modes, which are used for different purposes.

    Edit mode

Command mode

Visual edit mode

Extended command mode

When you first launch Vim, it will open in the command mode.

The command mode is useful for navigation, cut and paste jobs, and other tasks related to manipulation of text.

To enter the other modes of Vim, you need to enter single keystrokes, which are specific to every mode.

- If you use the i keystroke in the command mode, you will be taken to the insert mode, which lets you edit the text file.

    All content you type in the insert mode becomes a part of the file.

    You can return to the command mode by pressing the Esc key on the keyboard

- If you use the v keystroke in the command mode, you will be taken to the visual mode, where you can manipulate text by selecting multiple characters.

    You can use V and Ctrl+V to select multiple lines and multiple blocks, respectively.

You can exit the visual mode by using the same keystroke that is v, V, or Ctrl+V.

- The : keystroke takes you to the extended command mode, which lets you save the content that you typed to the file and exit the vim editor.

There are more keystrokes that are available in vim for advanced tasks related to text editing.

Although it is known to be one of the best text editors in Linux in the world, it can get overwhelming for new users.

We will go through the minimum keystrokes that are essential for anyone using vim to accomplish editing tasks in Linux.

Let us go through the steps given below to get some hands-on experience of vim for new users.

- Open a file on the shell prompt using the command *vim filename.*

- Repeat the text entry cycle given below as many times as possible until you get used to it.

- Use the arrow keys on the keyboard to position the cursor

- Press **i** to go to insert mode

- Enter some text of your choice

- You can use **u** to undo steps taken on the current line that you are editing

- Press the **Esc** key on the keyboard to return to the command mode

- Repeat the following cycle, which teaches you to delete text, as many times as possible, until you get the hang of it.

- Position the cursor using the arrow keys on the keyboard

- Delete a selection of text by pressing **x** on the keyboard

- You can use **u** to undo steps taken on the current line that you are editing

- You can use the following keystrokes next to save, edit, write or discard the file.

- Enter **:w** to save/write the changes you have made to the file and stay in the command mode

- Enter **:wq** to save/write the changes to the file and exit Vim

- Enter **:q** to discard the changes that you have made to the file and exit Vim

Chapter 15: Linux Softwares to Use

If you are going to start using Linux, one of the first things that you will need is a good selection of software.

In fact, many people stick with operating systems they hate, simply because they are hesitant to give up their favorite applications.

All of the software listed below are completely free and free to distribute to your friends or family.

That should help to convince you that using Linux is a great idea.

You can actually run Windows software in Linux, using a program called Wine.

However, you will basically be making your computer pretend to be using Windows.

If you would prefer to use dedicated, and often more reliable, methods — you are going to need some great Linux software.

Microsoft Word Alternatives

One of the most widely used tools in the business world is Microsoft Office.

Not long ago, if you were to apply for an office job without any knowledge of MS Office, you just might be laughed out of the room.

This might still be the case in many companies.

However, the days when MS Office was the one-and-only office suit are in the past.

Here are some great alternatives for Microsoft Office that run on Linux:

- OpenOffice. This wonderful, free, opensource office suite runs on Linux, Windows, and Mac OS. Consequently, you will find many people who use it, and it is largely compatible with MS Office documents.

You don't have to install the entire suite, but it contains software for word processing, spreadsheets, graphics, presentations, and databases.

If you just want something that will let you get on with your office work, and you only want to try one office suite for Linux — make it OpenOffice.

- LibreOffice. This one is based on OpenOffice, but the two makers separated in 2010.

It is a little less feature-rich than OpenOffice but will run better on slower machines.

That makes it a great choice for businesses using old computers.

Because of the small file size of LibreOffice, it can be installed on a USB drive and used on different computers.

- Google Docs. This is a very popular online office suite that ties in nicely with the rest of Google's online products.

If you already use a Google account, you will not need to do anything but sign in.

You can change your settings to be able to work offline, via your Internet browser, so Google Docs is no longer "online only."

Internet Browsers

If you are using a computer these days, you probably need to be online in order to be productive.

Luckily, you have plenty of choices for Linux web browsers.

You can even use the most popular browsers in Linux, so you won't have to settle for something else.

Here are some great Linux web browsers that you can try:

- **Firefox.** This is one of the most popular web browsers for Linux users.

There are faster options out there, as well as newer ones, but Firefox is considered one of the best.

- **Chrome.** You will need to download this from Google, as it won't be in the software repositories.

However, you can use Chromium instead, if you insist on using the repositories.

This is the number one web browser at the moment, and you will glad to know that Google fully supports Chrome for Linux.

- **In-built browsers.** Whatever version of Linux you choose, it will almost definitely come with a web browser, and that might even be Firefox or Chromium.

If you are not fussy about what you use, and just need to check websites every-now-and-then, you might be happy to use a default browser.

Audio, Video, and Image

If you want to be able to manipulate media files, whether creating a piece of art, recording a song, trimming down the video of your latest vacation, or just watching it — Linux has some create choices on offer.

- **GIMP.** If you want something to replace Photoshop, this is your best choice. However, there are some places where GIMP simply isn't as good as Photoshop.

- **PiTiVi.** If you want to do some basic home movie editing, this is a great choice of software.

While it will not give you the more professional functionality of Final Cut Pro, there are plenty of functions to choose from.

- **Audacity.** When it comes to working with sound files, this is the go-to application for Linux users.

With it, you can record multi-track audio files, cut them up, rearrange them, and add effects.

- **VLC.** This is a popular media player that is both powerful and reliable.

It will let you play more types of files than just about any other media player.

Email Clients

If you need your computer for work, you will probably want a good email client.

Windows users will probably be familiar with Outlook, but there are some good alternatives for Linux.

- **Thunderbird.** This is made by Mozilla, the same company that brought you Firefox.

It is a lightweight, easy-to-use email client, with lots of different options.

- **KMail.** This is the default for KDE desktop environments.

It has loads of features, although you might take a bit of time to get used to its layout.

- **Evolution.** This generally comes with the GNOME desktop environment.

It will let you use Google Calendar right away, as well as Microsoft Exchange.

It looks good and is simple to use.

Instant Messengers

If you are used to staying in touch with people on your computer, it's important to keep that functionality when you swap over to Linux.

Here are some good IM applications that you can try:

- **Skype.** This is an extremely popular instant messenger, and many people would be unwilling to part with using it.

- **Pidgin.** This IM software has been around for a long time and lets you log onto Facebook, Yahoo, Google, and many other networks.

Conclusion

So, it looks like you've reached the end of this book. I guess you should take a moment and congratulate yourself.

At this point, you have enough basic information to get started and begin to dabble in the usage of your own Linux distribution that you have chosen, installed, and began to program.

Hopefully, you found the process of reading this book informative and useful to you as you made your way through it.

The material discussed can be quite dense if you are not technologically inclined, or if you have never really dabbled in tech-related systems before, but it is worthwhile to learn.

As a beginner, you should familiarize yourself with the Linux commands.

This is the most interesting thing with Linux.

One enjoys running the commands on the terminal, which gives different results.

The interesting thing with Linux is that it comes with various distributions, and the majority of the commands are universal in all of these distributions.

This provides one with an ease of transition from one transition to another.

However, it is good for you to know that each Linux distribution is developed for a group of targeted users, and it is designed and developed so that it can meet the demands of those users.

These calls for you to determine the kind of tasks that you want to perform with your Linux, and then choose the best distribution from there!

One thing is for sure; however—when you begin to utilize Linux, you are developing a series of skills that are essential to learning.

It can be beneficial to know how to work with computers, and you may even decide to take this from a project to a hobby, and eventually even a career if it is something that has interested you enough to keep exploring.

No matter what, however, what is important to remember is that you should make sure you stay up-to-date on your knowledge.

From here, you may be ready to install your own iteration of Linux, if you have not done so yet.

If this is where you are at in your process, good luck!

It is an exciting time when you are first beginning on this process, and you will surely enjoy it.

If you are unsure whether you are ready to take the plunge into downloading a distribution for yourself, maybe you would find interest in running a few different distros to test first, using the steps listed for you earlier in this book.

You can play around with the system, learning which you prefer and which you would rather avoid altogether, which may help you make your decision sooner.

No matter what you decide, however, keep in mind that this was an intro to the subject.

This book focused on providing you with the basic essentials to understanding what Linux is and how it works.

From here, you may choose to research the specialized distribution you are interested in.

You may begin to look into more of the uses that Linux offers and what you can do with the program.

No matter what you choose to do next, if you are willing to put in the time and energy, you will find yourself successful in your endeavors.

I wish you the best of luck!

Finally, if you found this book useful in any way, a review on Amazon is always appreciated!

www.ingramcontent.com/pod-product-compliance
Lightning Source LLC
Chambersburg PA
CBHW071358210526
45465CB00001B/148